Classic
Reflections
on Scripture

CLASSIC
REFLECTIONS
on SCRIPTURE

W. E. Vine

with reflections by
Gregory C. Benoit

THOMAS NELSON
Since 1798

NASHVILLE DALLAS MEXICO CITY RIO DE JANEIRO

Published in Nashville, Tennessee, by Thomas Nelson. Thomas Nelson is a trademark of Thomas Nelson, Inc.

Writing, editing, and design by Gregory C. Benoit Publishing, Old Mystic, CT. **GB**

Thomas Nelson, Inc. titles may be purchased in bulk for educational, business, fund-raising, or sales promotional use. For information, please e-mail SpecialMarkets@ThomasNelson.com.

ISBN: 978-1-4185-4921-3

Printed in the United States of America

12 13 14 15 QG 5 4 3 2 1

CONTENTS

Introduction ix

The Mysteries of Scripture

The Mystery of Christ 3

The Mysteries of Scripture 7

The Mystery of the Faith 13

The Mystery of the Deity of Christ 17

The Mystery of Godliness 23

The Mystery of the Gospel 27

The Mystery of the Hardening of Israel 31

    A Distinction 35

The Mystery of the Kingdom 39

    The Kingdom of Heaven 43

The Mystery of Resurrection Bodies 49

    The Last Trumpet 55

The Mystery of Babylon 59

The Mystery of Lawlessness 65

    The Man of Lawlessness 69

    The Restrainer 73

The Mystery of God's Will 79

    Union in Christ 83

The Completion of the Mysteries 87

For Further Study 91

The Four Women of Revelation

The Four Women of Revelation 95

Jezebel...99

    Jezebel and Ahab..103

Babylon 107

    Babylon and the Beast 111

A Woman Clothed with the Sun 115

    The Woman and the Male Child.................................121

    The Woman and the Dragon.....................................125

The Bride, the Lamb's Wife...131

    Concerning Christ and the Church 135

    The City's Temple 141

    The River and the Tree..145

    The Lamb and the Stone...149

For Further Study 153

The Whole Gospel

Sin 157

    The Nature of Sin 161

    Natural Will 165

    Independence of God 169

Repentance 173

    Another Term 177

    Repentance as Used of God 183

Redemption 187

For Further Study 191

Introduction

William Edwy Vine (1873–1949) was a British writer and teacher who is best remembered for his unique *Expository Dictionary of New Testament Words*. He was, however, a rather prolific author who wrote many books on Bible study and theology, always approaching his topics with the same precision and insight he brought to his famous dictionary. Most of these books are now out of print, to the modern reader's loss, due in part to his writing style, which is today considered old-fashioned and even sometimes confusing.

This book takes some of the rich insights from Vine's works and smoothes the syntax to be more accessible to the modern reader. These selections offer both theological explication of the Scriptures and practical application of biblical principles to everyday life. Each selection is followed by a reflection intended to help Christians take the Bible's wisdom and apply it to their lives, while also providing deep concepts for meditation and further study. The selections are primarily from *The Twelve Mysteries of Scripture*, "The Four Women of the Apocalypse" (found in *The Second Coming and the Last Days*), and *The Whole Gospel*, with supplementary information from Vine's New Testament commentaries and from his *Expository Dictionary of New Testament Words*.

The book is divided into sections that accord with Vine's original works, and each section includes an exhaustive list of references for further study on selected topics. With these resources, the book can be used both as a tool for personal reflection and a springboard to deeper examination of God's Word. The ultimate goal, however, is to help modern Christians to apply God's Word to our lives, that each of us might be increasingly transformed into the image of Christ.

The Mysteries

of Scripture

Section Contents

The Mystery of Christ

The Mysteries of Scripture

The Mystery of the Faith

The Mystery of the Deity of Christ

The Mystery of Godliness

The Mystery of the Gospel

The Mystery of the Hardening of Israel

    A Distinction

The Mystery of the Kingdom

    The Kingdom of Heaven

The Mystery of Resurrection Bodies

    The Last Trumpet

The Mystery of Babylon

The Mystery of Lawlessness

    The Man of Lawlessness

    The Restrainer

The Mystery of God's Will

    Union in Christ

The Completion of the Mysteries

For Further Study

The Mystery of Christ

For we do not have a High Priest who cannot sympathize with our weaknesses, but was in all points tempted as we are, yet without sin.

—Hebrews 4:15

SCRIPTURE: *1 Timothy 3*

God was "manifested in the flesh" (1 Timothy 3:16), and this statement directly declares Christ's deity. Furthermore, His pre-existence is also clearly implied. That which is manifested has been hidden previously. He "was with the Father and was manifested to us" (1 John 1:2). "And the Word became flesh and dwelt among us" (John 1:14). Identifying Himself with humanity (apart from sin), Christ took on flesh and blood. This was the first step toward His role as Mediator between God and man. That relationship could only be brought about fully by His death and resurrection.

He was also "justified in the Spirit" (1 Timothy 3:16). The Mediator, in order to atone for sin by His sacrifice, must Himself be sinless. The absence of all sin during the whole of His life has been proved in every possible way, His enemies themselves bearing witness. His was the spirit of holiness, of absolute freedom from all taint or defilement. "And you know that He was manifested to take away our sins, and in Him there is no sin" (1 John 3:5). Christ passed unscathed through the fire of fierce temptation.

But how was He justified? Not as we are. We are justified by grace as sinners, but He was justified in vindication of His sinlessness. Righteousness is *imputed* to us, but it was *inherent* in Him. To this the Father bore witness at His baptism and at His transfiguration, and completely vindicated His sinlessness by raising Him from the dead. Thus it was that God justified His Son, and thus was fulfilled the messianic prophecy of Isaiah: "He is near who justifies Me" (Isaiah 50:8). He was "declared to be the Son of God with power according to the Spirit of holiness" (Romans 1:4). That declaration was only consistent with His holiness. Every test was applied, and He was proved to be the Just One, the Holy One.

ᔛ 1 JOHN 3:5 ᔚ

to take away our sins: John's point in this passage is that Christ became man; He became incarnate—and He did so in order to take away our sins. This shows that sin is incompatible with the divine relationship of being children of God. John's focus here is not on the nature of the atonement but on the effect it should have in the lives of believers.

An entire book—an entire library—could be written about the mystery of Jesus Christ, or God become flesh, and the mere surface of its depths would merely be skimmed. Indeed, an entire book has been written on the subject, for every page of the Bible is intent upon bringing to mankind God's ultimate good news, the gospel of God embodied in His Son. This book, too, endeavors to plumb in some small way the depth of God's grace through Christ, as we examine man's condition, the Devil's opposition, and Jesus' gift of eternal redemption. But before we can begin such an examination, we must first understand two vital pieces of this mystery: the deity of Christ and His sinless life on earth.

Jesus, God's only begotten Son, came to earth for the specific purpose of paying the price for the sin of the human race. But in order for this to be accomplished, He could not have any debt of His own to pay. The sin of Adam condemned all his descendants to a debt that they could not pay, the debt of death brought about by sin. God's justice demanded payment in full for this debt, but it could only be paid by One who was Himself without sin. Jesus lived His entire life on earth in complete obedience to the will of the Father and committed no sin. This fact was testified by the writers of the New Testament (Hebrews 4:15), and even by the very people who condemned Him to death on the cross (John 18:38; 19:4, 6). But the most irrefutable proof of His sinless life came from the Father Himself: "And suddenly a voice came from heaven, saying, 'This is My beloved Son, in whom I am well pleased'" (Matthew 3:17).

Jesus did not inherit the debt of death because He was born of a virgin, not having a human father to impart the sin nature to Him. Any human being born from Adam—that is, every human being who ever has lived or ever will live, apart from Christ—inherits the sinful nature because God ordained a law at creation: like brings forth like. A cow can only give birth to a cow, and a sinner can only give birth to a sinner. Every descendant of Adam is born under the curse, born subject to death, born with no possibility of being redeemed from sin—no hope, that is, apart from Christ. The only One who could ever live a life free from sin is God Himself, and that is the reason God became a Man—the Man Christ Jesus.

The Mysteries of Scripture

Now to Him who is able to establish you according to my gospel and the preaching of Jesus Christ, according to the revelation of the mystery kept secret since the world began but now made manifest, and by the prophetic Scriptures made known to all nations, according to the commandment of the everlasting God, for obedience to the faith—to God, alone wise, be glory through Jesus Christ forever.

—Romans 16:25–27

SCRIPTURE: *Ephesians 3*

The word *mystery* in Scripture does not refer to something that is mysterious. On the contrary, it refers to something that is "made known," something that can be known only by divine revelation—it is knowledge which is beyond a person's natural powers of comprehension. These divine mysteries are made known only by God's Holy Spirit, and they are revealed in the time and manner which God alone decides.

When we use the word *mystery* today, we generally refer to some knowledge which has been withheld from us; but in Scripture a mystery is in fact "truth revealed." Thus, the Bible uses terms such as "made known," "manifested," "revealed," "preached," and "understand" in connection with divine mysteries. The following passages illustrate this principle:

The mystery which has been hidden from ages and from generations, but now has been revealed to His saints.

—*Colossians 1:26*

(By which, when you read, you may understand my knowledge in the mystery of Christ), which in other ages was not made known to the sons of men, as it has now been revealed by the Spirit to His holy apostles and prophets.

—*Ephesians 3:4–5*

Now to Him who is able to establish you according to my gospel and the preaching of Jesus Christ, according to the revelation of the mystery kept secret since the world began.

—*Romans 16:25*

In the ancient religion of the Greeks, *mysteries* consisted of a set of rites and ceremonies which were considered very sacred, and they were observed with the strictest secrecy. Membership of the societies which practiced them was open to any who desired to be initiated, and those who had passed through the initiation were known as "the perfected." Paul probably had this in mind when he said, "However, we speak wisdom among those who are *mature* [literally, *perfect*], yet not the wisdom of this age, nor of the rulers of this age, who are coming to nothing. But we speak the wisdom of God in a *mystery*, the hidden wisdom which God ordained before the ages for our glory. . . . Now we have received, not the spirit of the world, but the Spirit who is from God, that we might know the things that have been freely given to us by God" (1 Corinthians 2:6–7, 12, *italics added*).

ᔕ MYSTERY ᔕ

The word *mystery* as used in the New Testament refers to things that can be made known only by divine revelation, in a manner and at a time appointed by God, to those who are illuminated by His Holy Spirit.

This all stands in striking contrast to the methods of secrecy adopted by the priests of the Greek mysteries. As Paul wrote, "But we have renounced the hidden things of shame, not walking in craftiness nor handling the word of God deceitfully, but by manifestation of the truth commending ourselves to every man's conscience in the sight of God" (2 Corinthians 4:2).

Mystery novels, movies, and television programs are a popular and enduring type of fiction in which the reader or viewer uses his wits and intellect to unravel the "whodunit," trying to guess at the truth, which the fiction writer has tried hard to disguise. We also tend to use the word *mysterious* in reference to a thing or person about which we know very little. We frequently add a sense of romantic adventure to the word, as though the "mysterious person" has a deep secret that we yearn to unravel.

The Bible, however, does not use the word *mystery* in these ways. The dictionary helps us to understand the biblical meaning: "a religious belief based on divine revelation, especially a doctrine of faith involving difficulties which human reason is incapable of solving."[1] There are two important distinctions in the Bible's use of *mystery* versus our casual English use: 1) a biblical mystery cannot be understood by human reason, but requires God's direct revelation; 2) a biblical mystery is intended to become clear, in God's timing, unlike modern mystery stories, which are deliberately designed to confuse and mislead a reader or viewer.

God desires that all people should know and understand the mysteries of the Bible, because these mysteries actually reveal His character and His will. A modern mystery writer wants to confuse his readers, to mislead them away from the truth of the plot—but God desires to reveal truth completely to anyone willing to listen. Ultimately, God's truth is fully revealed in His Son, Jesus Christ. "I am the way, the truth, and the life," Jesus told His disciples. "No one comes to the

Father except through Me. If you had known Me, you would have known My Father also; and from now on you know Him and have seen Him" (John 14:6–7). All the mysteries of the Bible eventually lead us to Christ.

[1] *The New Shorter Oxford English Dictionary*, Lesley Brown, ed. (Oxford: Clarendon Press, 1993), p. 1,874.

The Mystery of the Faith

*Likewise deacons must be reverent, not double-tongued,
not given to much wine, not greedy for money, holding
the mystery of the faith with a pure conscience.*

—1 Timothy 3:8–9

Scripture: *1 Corinthians 2*

Paul tells us that one of the qualifications for deacons
is to hold "the mystery of the faith" in a good conscience (1
Timothy 3:9). This faith is the body of Christian doctrine,
"once for all delivered to the saints" (Jude 3). The faith was
revealed in the person and work of Christ, made clear by
the Spirit of God to His apostles, and recorded in the New
Testament. It had been kept secret by God in preceding ages,
until the advent of Christ Himself, and it is in Christ that all
doctrines of Scripture are centered.

There was "a fullness of the time" for the revelation of the
faith, and God chose the time when it would be fully revealed.
The doctrines pertaining to this faith had been dimly fore-
shadowed in the Old Testament, but the clear revelation of
the mystery was brought about by Christ Himself in His days
on earth, and the revelation was completed by His apostles.

Paul refers to this as "the *mystery* of faith" because it
requires faith to fully comprehend it. Faith is a spiritual
activity rather than an intellectual exercise, because spiritual
understanding is required to comprehend spiritual truths.

Human intelligence alone cannot understand the mysteries of God, as Paul tells us: "But the natural man does not receive the things of the Spirit of God, for they are foolishness to him; nor can he know them, because they are spiritually discerned" (1 Corinthians 2:14).

Understanding the mystery of the faith is essentially the work of the Spirit of God, and He prepares the heart to receive it. Indeed, the very first step in comprehending this mystery is the act of accepting Christ *by faith*, on the spiritual understanding that His sacrifice on the cross was the only means of forgiveness for sins.

✌ FAITH ✌

The Greek word translated *faith* is *pistis*, meaning "firm persuasion." It is used in the New Testament of faith in God, Christ, or spiritual things. (See the list at the end of this section for all the passages where this word is used.)

All these things illustrate the nature of a scriptural mystery. There was first a period of "divine reticence," a time when God chose not to reveal the full plan of mankind's salvation. Next, there was an appointed time for the revelation of the mystery, through the coming of Christ and the commission of His disciples, who more fully explained those mysteries. And finally, the mystery was fully explained to the "chosen few," those who were specially prepared to receive the knowledge—in this case, any person who accepts the gospel of Christ through the work of the Holy Spirit.

Paul urged Timothy to teach others to be "holding the mystery of the faith with a pure conscience" (1 Timothy 3:9). The context of this statement was in choosing deacons, but the principle applies to all believers, whether or not we have been called to be deacons or elders within the church. But what does it mean in practical terms to be "holding the mystery of the faith"?

Vine points out two important elements of this process. First, Vine writes, "This faith is the body of Christian doctrine." The process of holding the mystery of the faith first requires that a Christian be well grounded in Christian doctrine. This can only come through an ongoing discipline of personal Bible study, meditation, and prayer, coupled with sound biblical teaching through regular participation in the local church. Second, Vine adds, "The faith was revealed in the person and work of Christ." This is perhaps the most important element in holding the mystery of the faith: walking in a close, obedient relationship with Jesus Himself. People learn best by imitation, and one can only imitate another person by spending time in close fellowship with that person.

Finally, as Paul reminded Timothy, one must have a "pure conscience," which can only be gained through diligent obedience to the Word of God and a regular habit of confessing sins when we fall short. This process of walking with Jesus and maintaining a pure conscience enables God's Holy Spirit to transform us into the image of Christ by renewing our minds and purifying our lives (Romans 12:1–2). And this transformation is critical to fully understanding and holding on to the mystery of the faith. As Paul reminded the Corinthians, "The natural man does not receive the things of the Spirit of God, for they are foolishness to him; nor can he know them, because they are spiritually discerned" (1 Corinthians 2:14).

The Mystery of the Deity of Christ

That their hearts may be encouraged, being knit together in love, and attaining to all riches of the full assurance of understanding, to the knowledge of the mystery of God, both of the Father and of Christ, in whom are hidden all the treasures of wisdom and knowledge.

—Colossians 2:2–3

SCRIPTURE: *Colossians 2*

Two mysteries involve doctrines concerning the Son of God: the mystery of God, and the mystery of godliness. The first is described as "the mystery of God, both of the Father and of Christ" (Colossians 2:2). This mystery refers to a duality within God's nature—that is, the Godhead is composed of two distinct persons, both Father and Christ. (The complete revelation of this mystery shows us that, in fact, the Godhead is composed of three distinct persons: Father, Son, and Holy Spirit—the Divine Trinity.) This divine unity, that multiple entities compose a single unified God, is beyond human understanding; the mystery can only be revealed by the special revelation of God.

But Christ came to give that revelation to all mankind. Early in His ministry, He declared that "no one knows the Son except the Father. Nor does anyone know the Father except the Son, and the one to whom the Son wills to reveal Him" (Matthew 11:27). He bore testimony to the Pharisees concerning His perfect unity with the Father when He declared, "I and My Father are one" (John 10:30). His disciples heard Him pray to the Father on their behalf, "Holy Father, keep through Your name those whom You have given Me, *that they may be one as We are.* . . . And the glory which You gave Me I have given them, *that they may be one just as We are one*" (John 17:11, 22, *italics added*).

John introduces Christ as the Revealer of God's mystery, the One who openly declares the truth which was once hidden: "No one has seen God at any time. The only begotten Son, who is in the bosom of the Father, He has declared Him" (John 1:18).

ᔐ COLOSSIANS 2:2 ᔐ

knit together in love: The verb *sumbibazō* means "to join, knit together; to be compacted, united." The Greek word *agapē* *(love)* is the characteristic word of Christianity. It speaks first of God's love and that of Christ, and then of Christian love, first toward God and then toward fellow believers, or toward men generally. It is to be distinguished from *affection (philia)*, which is used only in James 4:4.

In Colossians 2:3, Paul expounds on Christ's role as the Revealer of God's mysteries when he declares that "in [Christ] are hidden all the treasures of wisdom and knowledge." Christ is the Source of all God's revelation; all that God wishes to reveal to mankind is made clear in Jesus. Paul's aim in this epistle is to explain the deity, majesty, and power of the Son of God and to show us that all our needs are fully supplied through His redemptive sacrifice on the cross and His eternal role as our Redeemer and Lord.

The fullness of the Godhead is not something that was bestowed upon the Son, nor did Christ ever "assume deity." The fullness of deity was in Him from before creation, and it remained in Him when He became a man. In Christ, perfect humanity and absolute deity are completely combined. Paul emphasizes this when he declares, "For in Him dwells all the fullness of the Godhead bodily" (Colossians 2:9). His word *fullness* means "totally full," a fullness which existed from eternity past rather than a "filling up" of something that was not previously full.

This, then, is the mystery into which we are to enter, with "all riches of the full assurance of understanding" (Colossians 2:2). This, however, is not a blind acceptance of doctrine, but an appreciation of the glory and power of the Son of God which will guard us against being deluded into the many errors concerning Him, and from "not holding fast to the Head" (Colossians 2:19).

The deity of Christ is a central doctrine of the Christian faith. If Jesus is not God, then He has no authority to forgive sins, and the Christian's hope of redemption is in vain. The scribes and Pharisees recognized the importance of this doctrine—and they were the very men who opposed Jesus at every turn. One day, some people brought to Jesus a man who was paralyzed, and Jesus said, "'Son, your sins are forgiven you.' And some of the scribes were sitting there and reasoning in their hearts, 'Why does this Man speak blasphemies like this? Who can forgive sins but God alone?'" (Mark 2:5–7). The scribes were correct in their reasoning, insofar as it went, for to claim the authority to forgive sins is to claim to be God, and anyone other than Jesus would have been committing blasphemy with such a statement.

Jesus' claim to deity was not a side issue with His opponents; it was one of the reasons He was crucified. His enemies sought to kill Him when He healed the sick on the Sabbath, but their rage was vastly intensified by His claims to forgive sin. "Therefore the Jews sought all the more to kill Him, because He not only broke the Sabbath, but also said that God was His Father, making Himself equal with God" (John 5:18). The world frequently claims that Jesus was crucified because He was a good man, as though He was murdered for doing good and working miracles. Jesus said, "'I and My Father are one.' Then the Jews took up stones again to stone Him. Jesus answered them, 'Many good works I have shown you from My Father. For which of those works do you stone Me?' The Jews answered Him, saying, 'For a good work we do not stone You, but for blasphemy, and because You, being a Man, make Yourself God'" (John 10:30–33).

One of the key mysteries of Scripture is the triune nature of God, how God can be three entities of Father, Son, and Holy Spirit, all equal in godhead, yet all distinct. This mystery is coupled with another: how God could make Himself a man and be born of human flesh—born for the specific purpose of dying on the cross. Such mysteries cannot be comprehended by the mind of man, yet they are nonetheless true. As we come to know Jesus more fully, we are coming to know the fullness of God, and this is one of the most eternally precious aspects of being born again into Christ.

The Mystery of Godliness

And without controversy great is the mystery of godliness:
God was manifested in the flesh, justified in the Spirit,
seen by angels, preached among the Gentiles, believed on
in the world, received up in glory.

—1 Timothy 3:16

SCRIPTURE: *1 Timothy 4*

We are now to consider the second mystery relating to
the Son of God, called "the mystery of godliness," which Paul
describes as unquestionably great. To understand why this is
termed "the mystery of godliness," we must first understand
the greater context of 1 Timothy 3:9 through 4:7. At this point
in his letter to Timothy, Paul is discussing the testimony
which the church is called to give to the world. He has just
pointed out that overseers and deacons should have a good
testimony with the world around them, and now he is giving instructions on how men ought to behave in the house
of God.

He is concerned with the conduct of believers, as those
who constitute the house of God, in bearing witness to the
world, whether by word or deed. Then, beginning in 4:1,
Paul moves to the future, warning his readers concerning the
coming ungodliness and departure from the faith through
seducing spirits and doctrines of demons.

A church is the witness of God to men, and the essential elements of this witness are the truths concerning Christ, and especially those bearing upon the relations between God and man. The doctrines are not stated merely as so many concrete facts concerning Him; they form the basis of testimony as to godliness. And for such a testimony, godliness is essential. Thus, the truths which the apostle states concerning *Christ* form the climax to the exhortations that he has been giving concerning *godliness*. Truths which set forth the relations of God to man cannot be proclaimed by the church of the living God unless those within the church live "in all godliness" (1 Timothy 2:2).

✌ 1 TIMOTHY 3:16 ✌

manifested in the flesh: This refers both to the birth of Christ and His life on earth in the days of His flesh (all of which is really included in the term "incarnation"). It should be noted that the verb *phaneroō (to manifest)* implies the preexistence of the person who is the subject of the sentence; here, therefore, the statement involves the deity of Christ.

Personal godliness is of vital and absolute importance in the life of every Christian because godliness is the most powerful testimony of God's saving grace to the world around us. The old adage holds true: actions speak louder than words. A believer's words about Jesus might speak softly to his neighbor, but his actions are shouting, demonstrating the extent to which the believer actually believes the words he speaks, because godliness is an outward demonstration of one's inward faith in the Word of God.

Paul gives us a list in 1 Timothy 3 of what godliness looks like. Here are a few highlights:

- blameless
- temperate (not given to excess)
- hospitable
- able to teach
- gentle
- not greedy
- not quarrelsome
- not covetous

Paul further warns Timothy that the Devil, the enemy of our souls, is deliberately striving to lure men and women away from godliness, and that the day is coming when believers themselves will be seduced away from godliness and into false doctrines (1 Timothy 4:1). The essential step for believers who want to guard their lives for Christ is exercise:

exercising godliness even more diligently than one exercises physically. Paul urged Timothy to "exercise yourself toward godliness. For bodily exercise profits a little, but godliness is profitable for all things, having promise of the life that now is and of that which is to come" (1 Timothy 4:7–8). The way that one exercises godliness is to start by imitating Jesus, for His life on earth was the physical revelation of the mystery of godliness (1 Timothy 3:16). The more we exercise ourselves in godliness, the more we become like Christ.

The Mystery of the Gospel

And take the helmet of salvation, and the sword of the Spirit, which is the word of God; praying always with all prayer and supplication in the Spirit, being watchful to this end with all perseverance and supplication for all the saints—and for me, that utterance may be given to me, that I may open my mouth boldly to make known the mystery of the gospel, for which I am an ambassador in chains; that in it I may speak boldly, as I ought to speak.

—Ephesians 6:17–20

SCRIPTURE: *Ephesians 6*

Paul asked the believers in Ephesus to pray that the Lord would give him the words to speak and the boldness to speak them, making known the mystery of the gospel (Ephesians 6:18, 20). It was one of the chief subjects about which he had written to them.

Human intelligence or wisdom could never have conceived the truths of the gospel or the mystery relating to it. The truth was revealed to Paul by divine revelation, and the leading feature of it was "that the Gentiles should be fellow heirs, of the same body, and partakers of His promise in Christ through the gospel" (Ephesians 3:6). This, he says, had been hidden from men until God's time came for revealing it to His apostles and prophets (Romans 16:25–26). Paul speaks of the special revelation and trust given to him: "To me, who am less than the least of all the saints, this grace was given, that I should preach among the Gentiles the unsearchable riches of Christ, and to make all see [or perhaps "to bring to light to"] what is the fellowship of the mystery, which from the beginning of the ages has been hidden in God" (Ephesians 3:8–9).

✂ MYSTERY ✂

In the ordinary sense, a *mystery* implies knowledge withheld, but its scriptural significance is *truth revealed*. The terms especially associated with the subject of *mysteries* are "made known," "manifested," "revealed," "preached," "understand," "dispensation."

The wisdom of God is seen in the particular time appointed for the declaration of this mystery. To bring gentiles into spiritual union with Jews prior to the grace which we obtained through the sacrifice of Christ would have nullified the very purposes for which the law was ordained. The wall of separation between Jew and gentile had been built up by God, and that separation had to be maintained. Yet even while the wall was in existence, blessing for the gentiles was foretold from time to time, a matter to which Paul directs attention in Romans 10:18–20. The mystery was withheld relating to breaking down that barrier and incorporating believing Jews and gentiles into the one body of Christ, until the divine purposes of the law had been fulfilled and the message of salvation through faith in Christ could be sent to all men.

God chose Abraham and his descendants for the purpose of revealing His grace and truth to the entire human race. His larger purposes were for the blessing of all mankind, yet the family of Abraham received special blessings that were not available to others. God made His presence very real to the Jews, choosing to make His earthly dwelling in their midst as they journeyed from Egypt (Exodus 29:45) and after they had settled in the promised land (Psalm 26:8). God revealed His will and holiness to the descendants of Abraham by giving them the Law on Mount Sinai and by sending prophets to each generation, guiding them in a unique way into holiness and blessings. He brought the Messiah into the world through the seed of Abraham, bringing to fulfillment the picture of obedience and sacrifice, which Abraham himself portrayed when he was willing to sacrifice Isaac (Genesis 22).

The gentile nations—which is to say, all other nations on earth—did not enjoy this special relationship with God. Those who wanted to know more about the Creator of the universe, those who wanted to find atonement for sin or blessings for eternity, had to look to Israel for enlightenment. For a gentile, there was no special revelation of God's character, no provision for atonement, no blessings of His presence and guidance apart from moving to Israel and becoming a sojourner among the Jews—and even then, the gentile had limited access into God's presence, permitted only to enter the outer court of the temple.

All this was changed through Christ, for He has opened the way for all people to enter the presence of God. Indeed, anyone who is redeemed in Christ is given access into the holiest of holies, a place that was formerly not available to anyone, Jew or gentile, except the Jewish high priest alone. The blessings and revelations of God that were formerly available only to the descendants of Abraham are now freely available to anyone who has accepted God's final sacrifice through Jesus Christ His Son—"that the Gentiles should be fellow heirs, of the same body, and partakers of His promise in Christ through the gospel" (Ephesians 3:6).

The Mystery of the Hardening of Israel

For I do not desire, brethren, that you should be ignorant of this mystery, lest you should be wise in your own opinion, that blindness in part has happened to Israel until the fullness of the Gentiles has come in.

—Romans 11:25

SCRIPTURE: *Romans 11*

In Romans 1 through 10, Paul declares the absolute sovereignty of God in His designs and dealings and shows how His admission of gentiles into the blessings of salvation was consistent with His pledges to Israel. Paul then proceeds in Romans 11 to prove that God has not cast off His ancient people, the Jews. First, He has not cast them off totally. Paul himself is an Israelite, an example of the fact that "there is a remnant according to the election of grace," just as there was a remnant of faithful ones in Elijah's day (Romans 11:1–6).

Second, He has not cast them off forever. The rest of the nation are hardened and are suffering the consequences of "a spirit of stupor" (v. 8), yet their condition is not irretrievable. On the contrary, "through their fall . . . salvation has come to the Gentiles" (v. 11). And, so far from absolutely rejecting them, God has done this to provoke them to jealousy (vv. 7–11).

Third, their deliverer shall yet come and turn away their ungodliness. And if their temporary rejection has meant reconciliation for gentiles, how much greater will be the result of their own reconciliation! The nation is still the Lord's. The root of the olive tree is holy, so the branches are, too. Some have been broken off, and others have been grafted in. Then how much more shall the natural branches be grafted into their own tree!

ᔄ MYSTERIES IN SCRIPTURE ᔄ

The Greek word translated *mystery* is used to describe 1) spiritual truth; 2) Christ; 3) the church; 4) the rapture; 5) the hidden forces that work toward or against the kingdom of heaven; 6) the cause of the present condition of Israel; 7) the spirit of disobedience to God; 8) the seven local churches and their angels, seen in symbolism; and 8) the ways of God in grace.

In the previous reflection, we considered the fact that God opened the way for gentiles to enter His presence, a privilege that formerly was reserved only for the descendants of

Abraham. In the mystery of the hardening of Israel, however, we discover that this way was opened in part by the very fact that the people of Israel rejected Christ as Messiah. "Through their fall, to provoke them to jealousy," Paul states, "salvation has come to the Gentiles" (Romans 11:11). This is not to say, of course, that God deliberately caused the Jews to reject Christ; rather, He used their sinful hardness of heart to make His grace available to the entire human race.

The encouraging part of this mystery is the fact that God can use even the sinfulness of men to further His own purposes and grace. The enemies of Christ thought that they would put an abrupt end to His ministry when they crucified Him, but God simply used that deed to bring glory to His Son. Yet there is also a sobering element to this mystery: if God did not spare the descendants of Abraham when they hardened their hearts to His will, He will not spare others who follow that path—including those who have been redeemed by Christ's blood. As Paul warns us, "Do not be haughty, but fear. For if God did not spare the natural branches, He may not spare you either. Therefore consider the goodness and severity of God: on those who fell, severity; but toward you, goodness, if you continue in His goodness. Otherwise you also will be cut off" (Romans 11:20–22).

This does not mean that a Christian can lose his salvation. The Jews also have full opportunity to receive the grace of God through Christ: "And they also, if they do not continue in unbelief, will be grafted in, for God is able to graft them in again" (Romans 11:23). Paul is not speaking here of eternal separation from God but of the heavy hand of God's discipline on those who harden their hearts. Being born again into Christ secures a person eternal salvation, but God still commands that the believer continue to grow, to build a life of holiness upon the foundation of Christ's redemption. As Paul puts it, "Now if anyone builds on this foundation with gold, silver, precious stones, wood, hay, straw, each one's work will become clear; for the Day will declare it, because it will be revealed by fire; and the fire will test each one's work, of what sort it is. If anyone's work which he has built on it endures, he will receive a reward. If anyone's work is burned, he will suffer loss; but he himself will be saved, yet so as through fire" (1 Corinthians 3:12–15).

The Mystery of the Hardening of Israel

A Distinction

I say then, have they stumbled that they should fall? Certainly not! But through their fall, to provoke them to jealousy, salvation has come to the Gentiles.

—Romans 11:11

SCRIPTURE: *James 1*

The fullness of the gentiles is not quite the same thing as the church. For those Jews who have accepted Christ have already become part of the church, and they are distinguished from gentiles in Romans 11—though there is neither Jew nor gentile in Christ. Paul is not here speaking of the church, but of the dispensational dealings of God with Jew and gentile: of His judicial severity toward the Jews, His goodness toward the gentiles, and the common blessing held out to all. Paul also shows that Israel's salvation is subsequent to God's present mercy to gentiles: "For as you [that is, gentiles] were once disobedient to God, yet have now obtained mercy through their disobedience, even so these also have now been disobedient [literally, *these now have been disobedient to your mercy*], that through the mercy shown you they also may obtain mercy" (Romans 11:30–31). God's holy designs and sovereign will condition the motives and actions of humanity.

Mercy is the paramount theme in Romans 11. There is no salvation by works, either for gentile or Jew, for individual or nation. "For God has committed them all to disobedience, that He might have mercy on all" (Romans 11:32). Who can refrain from joining in Paul's doxology (vv. 33–36) once one has experienced the saving mercies of our God, looking forward to the day of Israel's deliverance and the glory of Israel's Messiah?

⅋ ROMANS 11:11 ⅋

to provoke them to jealousy: The conversion of the gentiles was intended to arouse the Jews to emulation of the gentiles' repentance and to a desire that they themselves might recover divine favor—not to stir them to jealousy in the ordinary sense of the word.

In the mystery of Israel's hardness, we also encounter a deeper mystery: the sovereignty of God. Indeed, this aspect of God's character is beyond the comprehension of mankind, for God is utterly in control of all things, including the deeds of men—yet simultaneously He does not cause men to sin or even tempt them to do so. God in His sovereignty may permit a man to be tempted toward sin, but that man is still entirely accountable for his actions. As James puts it, "Blessed is the man who endures temptation; for when he has been approved, he will receive the crown of life which the Lord has promised to those who love Him. Let no one say when he is tempted, "I am tempted by God"; for God cannot be tempted by evil, nor does He Himself tempt anyone. But each one is tempted when he is drawn away by his own desires and enticed" (James 1:12–14).

Paul demonstrates in Romans 11 that God's sovereignty is absolute. God permitted the Jews to harden their hearts in order that He might open the way for the gentiles to receive His gift of grace—and that same sovereignty will also bring His grace to the unbelieving Jews. In this sense, as Vine points out above, the Jews have been disobedient—to the mercy of the gentiles; that is, their disobedience is to the gentiles' advantage. Paul connects this concept with the fact that God's grace is entirely dependent upon God's own character; it has nothing to do with man's works, whether good or bad. God used the hardness of Israel to bring grace to the gentile, and He will also use the gentiles to bring grace to the Jews. "Even so then, at this present time there is a remnant according to the election of grace. And if by grace, then it is no longer of works; otherwise grace is no longer grace. But if it is of works, it is no longer grace; otherwise work is no longer work" (Romans 11:5–6).

This indeed is a deep mystery, past finding out! The human heart cannot hope to fathom it; we can only respond like Paul: "Oh, the depth of the riches both of the wisdom and knowledge of God! How unsearchable are His judgments and His ways past finding out! 'For who has known the mind of the LORD? Or who has become His counselor?' or who has first given to Him and it shall be repaid to him?' For of Him and through Him and to Him are all things, to whom be glory forever. Amen" (Romans 11:33–36).

The Mystery of the Kingdom

> *But when He was alone, those around Him with the twelve asked Him about the parable. And He said to them, "To you it has been given to know the mystery of the kingdom of God; but to those who are outside, all things come in parables."*

—Mark 4:10–11

SCRIPTURE: *Mark 4*

The mystery of the kingdom forms the subject of the parables recorded in Matthew 13, Mark 4, and Luke 8. In Matthew, the Lord speaks of the mysteries of the kingdom of heaven (literally, "of the heavens"); in Luke, "of the kingdom of God"; in Mark, they are summed up as "the mystery of the kingdom of God." The terms "the kingdom of God" and "the kingdom of heaven" are frequently interchangeable (e.g., Matthew 19:23, 24).

"The kingdom of God" is a general term for the kingdom in all its aspects, whether viewed in the past eternity, during the periods of human rebellion prior to the rejection of Christ, in the present age in which the kingdom is in mystery, or in the coming age when it will be made manifest. The term "kingdom of heaven" implies that there is another kingdom, one that is in opposition to God's sovereignty. The phrase "the kingdom of heaven" is confined to Matthew's gospel, where it occurs some twenty-five times, and Matthew's use of the term calls constant attention to the existence of antagonistic forces. Those forces are prominent in the parables of Matthew 13, which address the present time when the kingdom is in mystery. The fact that it is a mystery is due to the rejection of the King by the Jews. For this, they were temporarily cast away (Romans 11:15), and the kingdom was offered instead to men of every nationality.

↶ PARABLES ↷

The Greek word translated *parable* is *parabole*, which literally means "a placing of one thing beside another" in order to compare them. It generally refers to a story that is drawn from nature or human circumstances, the object of which is to set forth a spiritual lesson. It is the lesson that is of value; the hearer must catch the analogy if he is to be instructed. Such a story uses earthly things to discover a spiritual meaning; it is distinct from a fable, which attributes to things what does not belong to them in nature.

Have you ever wondered why Jesus used parables—sometimes parables that can be hard to understand—to explain God's truth to His followers? The disciples asked Him this very question after He taught the parable of the sower and the different types of soil: "And the disciples came and said to Him, 'Why do You speak to [the Jewish crowds] in parables?' He answered and said to them, 'Because it has been given to you to know the mysteries of the kingdom of heaven, but to them it has not been given. For whoever has, to him more will be given, and he will have abundance; but whoever does not have, even what he has will be taken away from him. Therefore I speak to them in parables, because seeing they do not see, and hearing they do not hear, nor do they understand'" (Matthew 13:10–13).

At first glance, this may seem like a harsh teaching—that a person who already has will be given more, while the person who lacks will lose even what little he does have. But Jesus was referring to the special privileges the Jewish nation enjoyed in their relationship with God, and He was specifically addressing the fact that many of the Jews had chosen, of their own volition, to blind themselves to God's truth. Those self-blinded people were rejecting Him as God's chosen Messiah, and so the Messiah would be taken away from them. On the other hand, however, there were many who joyfully received Jesus as the Christ—and this number eventually included gentiles—and those were the ones to whom even more would be given.

The important fact to understand in Jesus' teaching is that a person's "having" or "not having" is entirely a matter of one's own choice. The person who receives God's truth, who receives God's plan of salvation through Christ, that person will be given vastly more. But he who rejects the Word of God will lose even what little he had to begin with. Jesus made this clear in His reference to Isaiah: "And in them the prophecy of Isaiah is fulfilled, which says: 'Hearing you will hear and shall not understand, and seeing you will see and not perceive; for the hearts of this people have grown dull. Their ears are hard of hearing, and their eyes they have closed, lest they should see with their eyes and hear with their ears, lest they should understand with their hearts and turn, so that I should heal them'" (Matthew 13:14–15). It is a very dangerous thing to willfully close one's eyes to the truth of God's Word.

The Mystery of the Kingdom

The Kingdom of Heaven

Another parable He put forth to them, saying: "The kingdom of heaven is like a man who sowed good seed in his field; but while men slept, his enemy came and sowed tares among the wheat and went his way."

—Matthew 13:24–25

Scripture: *Matthew 13*

The church is not the same as the kingdom of heaven. The church has its part in the kingdom but, when it is removed from earth, the operations of the kingdom will continue here. At the present time, Christendom may be said to possess the traits of the kingdom in its "mystery phase," in that it consists of all who make some acknowledgment of Christ. All this is evident in the parables that set forth the mysteries of the kingdom. In the parable of the sower, the general principles of the kingdom are symbolized in the picture of the gospel being sowed to the souls of men. In the parables of the tares, the mustard seed, and the leaven, the outward aspect of the kingdom is presented. In each, the forces of evil are seen at work.

And the Lord's explanations draw our attention to final issues. The tares are bound in bundles by the servants (perhaps indicating ungodly associations) and left in the field to be burned; the wheat is taken into the storehouse. The true are removed before judgment is executed on the false, the binding in bundles being a preparation for that. The saints are to possess the kingdom, but that does not take place until "all things that offend, and those who practice lawlessness" (Matthew 13:41) have been cast out of it. In the parables of the sower and the tares, the individual is especially in view; the parables of the leaven and the mustard seed present a larger picture of the church in general. The parables of the treasure and the pearl present the inward aspect of the kingdom, and bring into greater prominence the divine appreciation of that which is true and genuine. In the parable of the net, the principles of the kingdom and their operations are again viewed in their ultimate issues, evil being purged out of it.

Thus, the Lord unfolds the secret of the kingdom of heaven during the period in which it exists in mystery. Throughout this period, the forces of darkness work simultaneously with the kingdom of heaven, the forces of darkness operating from beneath and the kingdom from above. The earth is the immediate arena of this conflict, where Satan aims at absolute dominion. But the heavens bear rule, and the adversary will not ultimately triumph. The darkness will not overpower the light, for the King will intervene in

Person. Satan will be bound and consigned to the abyss, and his human instruments will be destroyed. The mystery phase will be over, and the kingdom of God will be in manifested glory. "Then the righteous will shine forth as the sun in the kingdom of their Father" (Matthew 13:43).

ᦓ PARABLES ᦓ

Jesus' parables most frequently convey truths connected with the kingdom of God. He withheld the meaning from His hearers as He did from the multitudes as a divine judgment upon the unworthy. Two dangers are to be avoided in seeking to interpret the parables in Scripture: that of ignoring the important features, and that of trying to make all the details mean something.

Jesus' parables in Matthew 13 paint vivid pictures of the responsibilities of His church on earth, including obedience, attention to His Word and the Holy Spirit, and strengthening one's faith. But one of the more sobering responsibilities is concern for one's neighbor, which Jesus illustrated in the parable of the wheat and tares (Matthew 13:24–30). The picture here is of a wheat field in which a farmer has worked diligently to plant and cultivate a wholesome crop, but the farmer's enemy has also been busy sowing weeds among the good wheat.

The *tares* referred to are probably a type of grass that grows in the Middle East, a worthless weed that looks very much like real wheat. The tares and wheat would be growing together side by side, making it difficult for the farmer to discern the crop from the weeds prior to the time of harvest; and even if he could discern the difference, he would have been unable to uproot the tares without also uprooting the intermingled wheat. Yet those tares still had to be separated from the wheat, because they would make a person sick if mixed together into the wheat flour.

The most moving portion of Jesus' parable is its conclusion, when the tares are gathered together and burned. The Lord was using this parable to explain to His disciples that a day of judgment is coming when the multitudes who have rejected His gift of salvation will be gathered together and separated from the redeemed, and they will be cast out from God's presence for all eternity. A Christian cannot ignore the terrible fate that awaits those who reject Christ, and this knowledge should help motivate Christ's followers to concern themselves with their unbelieving neighbors.

Yet believers must also expect to encounter opposition in sharing the gospel with others. Jesus underscored this in the parable, alerting His listeners to the fact that there is an enemy who skulks in the darkness, deliberately sowing lies. The farmer planted good seed, "but while men slept, his enemy came and sowed tares among the wheat and went his way" (Matthew 13:25). As Christ's representatives on earth, believers do well to remain alert to the efforts of the evil one, working to spread the gospel and preserve their neighbors from the coming fire.

The Mystery of Resurrection Bodies

Behold, I tell you a mystery: We shall not all sleep, but we shall all be changed—in a moment, in the twinkling of an eye, at the last trumpet. For the trumpet will sound, and the dead will be raised incorruptible, and we shall be changed.

—1 Corinthians 15:51–52

SCRIPTURE: *1 Corinthians 15*

We are now to consider the last of the group of mysteries connected with the church. The first, the mystery of the gospel, relates to its formation, while the last relates to its consummation: the resurrection of the saints—"for this corruptible must put on incorruption, and this mortal must put on immortality" (1 Corinthians 15:53). It should be observed that the resurrection itself is not a mystery. The Scriptures had revealed this truth many times before Paul wrote. Job knew that his body would be raised from the dead (Job 19:23–27), and so did David (Psalm 16:9–11; 17:15). The resurrection of saints was prophesied by Isaiah (Isaiah 25:8) and by Hosea (Hosea 13:14), and it was made known to Daniel (Daniel 12:2).

The Lord also predicted it in fuller detail, both publicly to the Jews (John 5:28–29; 6:39, 44) and privately to His disciples (11:24–26; 14:19). Martha's words to the Lord concerning Lazarus, "I know that he will rise again in the resurrection at the last day" (John 11:24), and the ironic reference by the Sadducees to "the resurrection" (Matthew 22:28, 30) show that the doctrine of the resurrection was commonly accepted, except by the sect of the Sadducees. The doctrine was regularly taught by the Pharisees (Acts 23:6, 8). It constituted an essential truth of the gospel preached by the apostles (Acts 4:2). And in 1 Corinthians 15, it is the subject of Paul's main argument.

↝ Resurrection ↝

The Greek word translated *resurrection* is *anastasis*, which means "a raising up" or "rising," literally "causing to stand up." See the end of this section for a complete listing of uses of this word in the New Testament.

Paul has something now to add beyond the fact that there will be a resurrection of the saints, something not previously made known: that not all the saints will fall asleep, but that the bodies of all will together be changed. This change involves resurrection for those whose bodies have died, but the point of the mystery is the simultaneous transformation of the bodies of all saints, whether or not they have passed through death. This was a new revelation, confirmed by the passage in 1 Thessalonians 4, where the apostle declares that it was made known to him by the word of the Lord; that is to say, not by the Scriptures, but by a revelation from the ascended Christ.

This particular truth, like the mystery of the body of Christ, seems to have been committed to Paul to be made known to the church. There is no indication of its having been revealed before. In 1 Thessalonians, we are taught that one event will follow another; first the resurrection of those who have fallen asleep, then the simultaneous rapture of all believers in Christ. In 1 Corinthians 15:51–53, the leading idea is the instantaneous transformation of all—the corruptible body which has died putting on incorruption, and the mortal body which has not yet experienced death putting on immortality, and all taking place "in a moment, in the twinkling of an eye."

In these passages, Paul gives us a short overview of both the origins of death and the importance of the resurrection. God created Adam to stand in the place of the entire human race as "the son of God" (Luke 3:38), but he chose to disobey the one commandment of God, thereby placing himself and the entire world under subjection to sin and death. This meant that every descendant of Adam—every person who has ever lived throughout the history of the world—is under the inescapable doom of death. But Jesus came as the Last Adam, the true Son of God, and He lived a completely sinless life. His death on the cross was voluntary, since He was not subject to death, and through it anyone can be "born again" (John 3:3) into the family of the Last Adam, thus being set free from death. Jesus' resurrection demonstrated the truth of this promise, proving that He and His spiritual "descendants" have victory over the grave. If Jesus had not been victorious over death, then His followers "are of all men the most pitiable" (1 Corinthians 15:19).

The resurrection of all believers in Christ is an absolute certainty, guaranteed both by the resurrection of Christ and by the indwelling of the Holy Spirit (1 Corinthians 15:20–22), and at that time we will be given new bodies that are free from sin and decay. But there is a responsibility that comes with this promise, for God commands His children to begin the work of sanctification here on earth while we occupy our present, corruptible bodies. Paul wrote of this to the believers in Thessalonica: "For this is the will of God, your sanctification: that you should abstain from sexual immorality; that each of you should know how to possess his own vessel in sanctification and honor" (1 Thessalonians 4:3–4). Our present bodies are destined for the grave, but our spirits will live for all eternity, and God calls us to sanctify ourselves now in preparation for that eternity.

This process of sanctification certainly involves avoiding sin, such as the sexual matters that Paul addresses in the verses cited above, but it is far more comprehensive than that. We are called to be like Christ, and this includes learning to love others as He loves us. "But concerning brotherly love," Paul writes, "you have no need that I should write to you, for you yourselves are taught by God to love one another.... But we urge you, brethren, that you increase more and more; that you also aspire to lead a quiet life, to mind your own business, and to work with your own hands, as we commanded you, that you may walk properly toward those who are outside, and that you may lack nothing" (1 Thessalonians 4:9–12). The future for all believers includes the glorious guarantee of an eternal resurrection; let us, therefore, begin to prepare for the future in the present.

The Mystery of
Resurrection Bodies

The Last Trumpet

*For the Lord Himself will descend from heaven with
a shout, with the voice of an archangel, and with the
trumpet of God. And the dead in Christ will rise first.*

—1 Thessalonians 4:16

SCRIPTURE: *Exodus 19*

The mystery of our resurrection bodies is to have fulfillment at the last trumpet, which is the only indication of
the time of the resurrection. It would be somewhat arbi-
trary to assume that this trumpet is the last in the series of
trumpets mentioned in Revelation 8, 9, and 11. The trumpets
of Revelation are symbolic, like the seals and vials, but in 1
Thessalonians 4:16, Paul is not speaking in the symbolism
of visions. His language, if figurative, is metaphorical rather
than symbolic. But 1 Corinthians 15:52 and 1 Thessalonians
4:16 suggest the actual sounding of a trumpet. Moreover,
the visions in Revelation came to John some time after
1 Corinthians was written.

The last trumpet may be a military metaphor and possibly has reference to the trumpets mentioned in Numbers 10:2–6, by which the people of Israel were assembled to move the camp. On the other hand, the "last trump" may stand in contrast with the trump of Sinai (Exodus 19). The subject of the law was so constant in the apostle's teaching that an indirect reference to the occasion would be readily grasped by the readers without further explanation. Also, the distinction between the "last trumpet" and a first trumpet is quite in keeping with the similar distinction given in 1 Corinthians 15:45 between "the first Adam" and "the last Adam," where only two men are in view, not a series of men. The first trumpet was an announcement of condemnation; the last will be an announcement of emancipation. The first proclaimed a curse and threatened death; the last will proclaim the blessing of eternal life. The first separated the terror-stricken hearers from the presence of God; the last will bring the saints to their Savior in the joy of perfect union.

☙ MYSTERY ❧

The Greek word translated *mystery* is *mystērion*. See the end of this section for a complete list of Scripture verses that use this word.

Early in their exodus from Egypt, the Israelites arrived at Mount Sinai, where God met with Moses (Exodus 19). The Lord made His presence palpable on that mountain, bringing Himself to His people in a physical sense, yet the people were not permitted to come anywhere near Him. On the contrary, nobody was even permitted to so much as touch the base of Sinai with the sole of their foot; anyone who did so, even animals, were to be put to death immediately. The presence of God was so holy that the people were not even permitted to touch a person who had touched the base of the mountain on which God had descended!

The Lord's presence, furthermore, was accompanied by terrifying signs: roaring thunder, crackling lightning, a dense cloud that obscured all sight, fire and smoke that threatened instant judgment, heat as if from a mighty furnace, an earthquake—and through it all, the ringing sound of a loud trumpet. These wonders are all associated with wrath and judgment, and many reappear in Revelation as indications of God's anger poured out upon the earth. Indeed, it was such a terrifying experience that all the people of Israel trembled in fear (v. 16).

The sound of a heavenly trumpet in Scripture is thus generally associated with the fierce wrath of God, and it is a sound to be dreaded. But one day, the very last trump shall resound throughout the earth, and God's people will rejoice, for it will herald the resurrection of the saints. This trumpet will be distinctly different from the one heard on Mount Sinai thousands of years ago. There will be no wrath, no judgment for the people of God. On the contrary, it will be a joyful reunion into the very presence of the Lord. The people of Israel at Sinai were not permitted to approach anywhere near to God's presence, but one day those redeemed through Christ will be gazing on the very face of our Creator. This final trumpet will declare for all the world that God's wrath has ended, because it was poured out in full on the person of His Son Jesus.

The Mystery of Babylon

And on her forehead a name was written: MYSTERY,
BABYLON THE GREAT, THE MOTHER OF HARLOTS AND
OF THE ABOMINATIONS OF THE EARTH.

—Revelation 17:5

SCRIPTURE: *Genesis 10*

In the vision recorded in Revelation 17, John was called
to behold "the judgment of the great harlot who sits on many
waters, with whom the kings of the earth committed fornication, and the inhabitants of the earth were made drunk with
the wine of her fornication" (Revelation 17:1–2). A woman
was seen, gorgeously arrayed, holding a cup of abominations,
and "sitting on a scarlet beast which was full of names of blasphemy, having seven heads and ten horns" (v. 3). Inscribed
upon her forehead was the title "Mystery, Babylon the Great,
the Mother of Harlots and of the Abominations of the Earth"
(v. 5). "I saw the woman," wrote John, "drunk with the blood
of the saints and with the blood of the martyrs of Jesus. And
when I saw her, I marveled with great amazement" (v. 6).

In the interpretation of some, the woman is identified
with Rome: "And the woman whom you saw is that great city
which reigns over the kings of the earth" (v. 18). In this view,
Rome was the seat of Babylonian-style evil. Yet the name of
the woman was associated with Babylon as a mystery, indicating that there were facts concerning Babylon which had

not yet been revealed and that the time had now come for the evils connected with it to be made known to the saints.

We must, therefore, review the origin and history of Babylon, a city that was built under sinister conditions. Babylon began as the city of Babel, recorded in Genesis 11, and the motives of its founders demonstrate that they did so regardless of God. Their designs were to establish a lasting monument to their energy and prowess, to make a name for themselves, and to resist God's command to "be fruitful and multiply, and fill the earth" (Genesis 9:1). To reckon without God is to court disaster, and divine retribution was speedy. Their language was confounded, their aims were thwarted, the building operations ceased, and the people were scattered (Genesis 11:1–9).

࿐ **MARTYR** ࿐

the martyrs of Jesus: The Greek word translated *martyr* is *martys* or *martyr*, meaning "one who bears witness, who testifies to what he has seen or heard or knows." It is used of God; of Christ; of those who bear witness for Christ by their death; and of the interpreters of God's counsels, who will one day bear witness in Jerusalem in the times of the antichrist.

The city shortly afterwards became the scene of a second attempt at unity, now in a different way, yet still without recognition of God. Nimrod was apparently the first man to set up a kingdom in the earth. Having won fame among his peers, he seems to have conceived the idea of repairing the disorder caused by the confusion of tongues by uniting men under himself. "And the beginning of his kingdom was Babel, Erech, Accad, and Calneh, in the land of Shinar" (Genesis 10:10). From there, he invaded Assyria, which belonged to the descendants of Shem, and built Nineveh and other towns (v. 11). Babel, however, was his capital. (The events recorded in Genesis 11:1–9 occurred prior to the events of 10:10–11. Chapter 10 is occupied with the genealogy of the descendants of Noah, while the opening of chapter 11 is an expansion on those details.)

The city of Babylon probably had its roots in the man named Nimrod, discussed in Genesis 10 and 11. We will see in a later reflection that Babylon figures large in the events of the end times, and we may learn some basic principles of godliness by considering the origins of that great city. As a general rule in Scripture, powerful gentile cities are shown to be centers of worldly corruption. The nations of Assyria, Nineveh, and Babel—all listed in chapter 10—are notorious for their wickedness, as seen within the pages of the Bible.

The name *Nimrod* can mean "the valiant one," and it can also mean "rebellion." The men of Nimrod's day focused on the first meaning, speaking of his valor and prowess as a hunter; but God was more concerned with the second meaning of his name, as his life "before the LORD" (literally, "*in* the Lord's face") was characterized by a spirit of rebellion (Genesis 10:9). It is important to remember, when reading the account of Babel in Genesis 11, that God had commanded Noah and his descendants to "be fruitful and multiply, and fill the earth" (Genesis 9:1). The Lord wanted people to spread out throughout the earth, not to congregate in one place. This does not mean that a city is inherently wrong in God's eyes; it has to do with the motives that led Nimrod and his followers to build their great city.

The people said to one another, "Come, let us build ourselves a city, and a tower whose top is in the heavens; let us make a name for ourselves, lest we be scattered abroad over the face of the whole earth" (Genesis 11:4). These words reveal several rebellious elements. First, the repetition of "ourselves," which indicates where the focus lay for all their plans and schemes: on the self, much like the cult of "self-esteem" in our world today. Second, the people of Babel did not trust God's sovereign protection; they foolishly thought that they would be safer if they banded together than if they obeyed God's command to fill the earth. Ironically, had they been obedient to God's command, they would have voluntarily spread over the globe, but by disobeying they ended up being "scattered" (v. 8)—the very thing they wanted to avoid.

Another rebellious element in the people's words was their desire to "make a name" for themselves. Their focus was on praising themselves for their accomplishments and independence rather than on praising and worshiping the God who created them. Finally, the people of Babel foolishly believed that they could raise themselves to heaven through the power of their own hands, and this attitude still persists in most of the world's religions today. Mankind cannot ever enter the presence of God through any efforts of his own, whether of deliberate good deeds, abstinence from evil, or attainment of some mystical goal. Only by submitting to the will and Word of God can any person ever enter His kingdom, and any effort in the other direction will inevitably lead to confusion and failure.

The Mystery of Lawlessness

Let no one deceive you by any means; for that Day will not come unless the falling away comes first, and the man of sin is revealed, the son of perdition . . . that he may be revealed in his own time.

—2 Thessalonians 2:3, 6

Scripture: *2 Thessalonians 2*

The mystery of lawlessness is addressed in 2 Thessalonians, in a passage in which Paul is correcting his readers' mistaken views concerning the coming of the Lord Jesus and the day of the Lord, and he draws a distinction between these two events or ages. He shows that the day of the Lord—a period of God's judgments in the earth—had not yet begun as they had been led to believe. Paul explains that certain events in the world must precede the day of the Lord—events connected with the mystery of lawlessness.

Before speaking of those events, we must consider the meaning of the phrase "the mystery of lawlessness." It does not indicate that the lawlessness referred to is something mysterious or something working in a mysterious way. There is no mystery, in the ordinary sense of the term, about lawlessness itself, which simply consists of the rejection of law, whether divine or human. The "mystery of lawlessness" is something more than this. Lawlessness is part of Satan's plan to overthrow God's government, as it is used in Scripture— that is, something which lies beyond human comprehension that can become known only by divine revelation. The spirit of independence from God and of refusal to accept His revealed will is directed by the prince of the power of the air "who now works in the sons of disobedience" (Ephesians 2:2). His aim is to shut out God, dethrone Christ, and exalt man in His place under his own control.

✜ LAWLESSNESS ✜

The mystery of lawlessness is not recognized by the world, for it does not consist merely of confusion and disorder. The display of lawlessness by the lawless one will be the effect of the attempt by the powers of darkness to overthrow the divine government. First John 3:4 states, "Whoever commits sin also commits lawlessness, and sin is lawlessness." This definition of sin sets forth its essential character as the rejection of the will of God and the substitution of the will of self.

How little do men realize that the arch-opponent of God is at the back of the world's movements, and he is goading men on to rebellion against the Most High and to its consequent judgment! Yet so it is. The truths of this mystery become increasingly clear to the one who bows to the authority of

Christ and intelligently reads the Scriptures—especially as he sees them confirmed by events in the world.

As we saw in our previous reflection, mankind possesses a spirit of rebellion in his very nature, stemming all the way back to the day when Adam rebelled against the single command of God (Genesis 3). But mankind is not alone in this rebellion; our race is constantly goaded and prodded to rebel against God by the Devil, the former angel who invented the concept of rebellion when he tried to make himself equal with God (Isaiah 14:12–15). The enemy of our souls works ceaselessly, day and night, urging men and women to disregard the laws of God and to become a law unto themselves.

Indeed, this was the very sin that Lucifer committed in heaven some time prior to his appearance in the garden of Eden. He said in his heart, "I will ascend into heaven, I will exalt my throne above the stars of God; I will also sit on the mount of the congregation on the farthest sides of the north; I will ascend above the heights of the clouds, I will be like the Most High" (Isaiah 14:13–14). God cast Lucifer down from heaven, and he immediately proceeded to seduce the human race into the same foolish thinking, seducing people into believing that they can only be truly free when they overthrow law and make their own rules. This trend is increasingly prevalent in the world today, both on the individual plane of setting "self" above all else, and on the social plane where we see increasing societal unrest resulting in riots and anarchy.

This trend will continue and intensify as the day of the Lord draws near. Paul warned Timothy, "But know this, that in the last days perilous times will come: For men will be lovers of themselves, lovers of money, boasters, proud, blasphemers, disobedient to parents, unthankful, unholy, unloving, unforgiving, slanderers, without self-control, brutal, despisers of good, traitors, headstrong, haughty, lovers of pleasure rather than lovers of God, having a form of godliness but denying its power. And from such people turn away!" (2 Timothy 3:1–5).

A generation such as Paul is describing will one day fill the earth with chaos, as each man strives to do what is right in his own eyes, each person acting as a law unto himself. Yet God's people should not lose heart, though the times might be increasingly evil. Jesus said, "And there will be signs in the sun, in the moon, and in the stars; and on the earth distress of nations, with perplexity, the sea and the waves roaring; men's hearts failing them from fear and the expectation of those things which are coming on the earth, for the powers of the heavens will be shaken. Then they will see the Son of Man coming in a cloud with power and great glory. Now when these things begin to happen, look up and lift up your heads, because your redemption draws near" (Luke 21:25–28).

The Mystery of Lawlessness

The Man of Lawlessness

And then I will declare to them, "I never knew you; depart from Me, you who practice lawlessness!"

—Matthew 7:23

SCRIPTURE: *Matthew 7*

Lawlessness is not necessarily characterized by confusion and disorder. Even religion and morality may be characterized by a rejection of God's counsels and claims, as made known in His Word, and they may themselves constitute lawlessness. This was taught by the Lord in the Sermon on the Mount. He showed that it is possible to call Him "Lord" and yet not to do the will of His Father (Matthew 7:22–23). Lawlessness is the disregard of the will of God. Self-will may either act along the moral and religious plane, or break out in openhanded rebellion against God. In each case, men are guilty of lawlessness.

Paul tells the Thessalonian saints that the day of the Lord (the period ushered in by the second coming of Christ) will not commence until the falling away has come (a general departure from God and His Word), "and the man of sin [literally, *man of lawlessness*] is revealed, the son of perdition, who opposes and exalts himself above all that is called God or that is worshiped, so that he sits as God in the temple of God, showing himself that he is God" (2 Thessalonians 2:3–4). He is called in verse 8 "the lawless one"—that is, he will be the very embodiment of lawlessness. The world, moreover, will be ripe to receive this emissary of Satan.

Meanwhile, the mystery of lawlessness was already working in Paul's time and has been working ever since—only it has been under restraint, and Paul states that this has been imposed in order that the Man of Sin may be revealed at the proper season. He describes the restraining power in two ways: first as a principle, "what is restraining" (v. 6); and second as a person, "He who now restrains" (v. 7). The person evidently embodies the principle. The restraint would continue until the power exercising it would be taken out of the way, the result being the revelation of the lawless one.

꒜ 2 THESSALONIANS 2:3 ꒜

Let no one deceive you: The Greek word translated *deceive* is *exapataō*, a word elsewhere used of the influence of sin and of self-deception. This warning exhortation is an echo of the words of the Lord, "Take heed that no one deceives you" (Matthew 24:4); indeed, Paul might well be translating and quoting what Jesus actually said.

Doing good works is not the solution to lawlessness. The evil of lawlessness is the natural outgrowth of pride, as we saw previously in the sin of Lucifer. It is the act of raising oneself to be equal with God, leading inexorably to the notion that one is free to make laws of right and wrong, which is the prerogative of God and His appointed authority structures. But this wicked attitude might very well be hidden under a mask of righteousness (which is actually self-righteousness), taking the form of things that seem good from the human perspective. The scribes and Pharisees were experts in this trickery, cloaking their spiritual pride in all manner of legalism. The Lord called these men "hypocrites," "witnesses against yourselves," and "vipers" (Matthew 23:29–33).

The solution to lawlessness is submission, and it is no coincidence that the concept of being submissive is treated with scorn and derision in our culture today. Jesus fully demonstrated submission in His life, yielding Himself entirely to the will of the Father—even to the point of going to the cross, though that obedience was at great cost to Himself. Submission is the opposite of pride, since one is effectively deeming others as better than oneself by the very act of submitting to that other person. This is what Paul had in view when he commanded his readers, "Let nothing be done through selfish ambition or conceit, but in lowliness of mind let each esteem others better than himself" (Philippians 2:3).

Jesus was very clear on the dangers of a prideful spirit, as a prideful spirit leads to lawlessness. He warned His disciples that His Father wants men to willingly submit themselves to His will, obeying His Word in a spirit of trust and humility: "Not everyone who says to Me, 'Lord, Lord,' shall enter the kingdom of heaven, but he who does the will of My Father in heaven. Many will say to Me in that day, 'Lord, Lord, have we not prophesied in Your name, cast out demons in Your name, and done many wonders in Your name?' And then I will declare to them, 'I never knew you; depart from Me, you who practice lawlessness!'" (Matthew 7:21–23).

The Mystery of Lawlessness

The Restrainer

For the mystery of lawlessness is already at work; only He who now restrains will do so until He is taken out of the way.

—2 Thessalonians 2:7

SCRIPTURE: *James 4*

In the last section, we encountered the restrainer, or "He who now restrains" (2 Thessalonians 2:7). There are two explanations concerning this restraining power. One is that the restrainer is the Holy Spirit, acting through the church; at the rapture of the church, the Holy Spirit will be taken away from the earth. The other explanation is that the restraining principle is that of constituted government, which is always embodied in the highest ruler in the state and was represented in Paul's time by the Roman emperor. The phrase "He who now restrains" is literally "the restrainer," and so the phrase might stand for a number of individuals presenting the same characteristics, just as "the believer" stands for all believers.

Such constituted authority is at all times a great restraining power against lawlessness, which is clear from facts of Scripture history (Acts 17:9; 18:12–17; 19:40; 21:27–36; 25:6–12); from the doctrine of Scripture (Romans 13:1–7; 1 Timothy 2:2; 1 Peter 2:13–17); and from facts of the history of nations up to the present day. When the government of any country has been overthrown by revolutionary mobs, lawlessness has broken loose from the great restraint which controlled it. So it was in the French Revolution. So it was in the recent history of Russia and Germany. Revolutionary socialism is merely a form of lawlessness that disregards the authority of God and would overthrow all forms of government that He has ordained for the maintenance of peace and order, retaining its power by anarchy. The evidence is abundant that, in Christendom itself, restraint is being thrown off and lawlessness is spreading rapidly. If constitutional government is overthrown in a still more general way, and the laws of God for man are repudiated still more widely, the situation will be fully ripe for the advent of the lawless one.

In whatever way lawlessness spreads, whether by anarchy or by bloodless revolutions, Satan is rapidly preparing the ground for the production of his human masterpiece. Whatever the restraining power may be—and it certainly appears to be considerably weakened at the present time—it will be removed, and the Man of Sin will arise to take control of men and world affairs.

His period of power will be brief. The Satanic scheme will be upset for the worldwide dominion of man, in rebellion against God and Christ. A Man who is stronger than the strong man will come and bind him and spoil his goods. "And then the lawless one will be revealed, whom the Lord will consume with the breath of His mouth and destroy with the brightness of His coming" (2 Thessalonians 2:8). Lawlessness will then yield to righteousness under the benign yet firm government of God's King, the Son to whom the Father says, "You have loved righteousness and hated lawlessness" (Hebrews 1:9). God hasten the day of His glory in the earth, when He shall reign in righteousness and justice from sea to sea!

✣ ROMANS 13:2 ✣

whoever resists the authority resists the ordinance of God: Civil government is God's design, and those who exercise it derive their authority from Him. Therefore, resistance to that authority is disobedience to God.

As we saw in the previous reflection, the solution to lawlessness is submission. There is a powerful paradox in the life and teachings of Christ, in the sense that the Devil is driven away, not through our great deeds of spiritual valor but through our meekness and submission. The reverse of this also holds true: when a believer insists on his own way, he becomes his own personal law-giver and ends up doing the Devil's work rather than God's. But when a believer submits himself fully to the will and sovereignty of God, the Devil is powerless.

This is not some "Gandhi-style" idea of passive-resistance; it is turning over all things to the power and authority of God, because God Himself dwells within every born-again follower of Christ. It is not a passive act at all but a very deliberate choice to allow God to fight our battles. "You are of God, little children, and have overcome them," Jesus told His disciples, "because He who is in you is greater than he who is in the world" (1 John 4:4). The Holy Spirit indwells all believers for the specific role (among other reasons) of restraining the enemy of our souls. James gives us clear instruction on how a believer is to submit himself to the Holy Spirit.

> Do you not know that friendship with the world is enmity with God? Whoever therefore wants to be a friend of the world makes himself an enemy of God. Or do you think that the Scripture says in vain, 'The Spirit who dwells in us yearns jealously'? But He gives more grace. Therefore He says: 'God resists the proud, but gives grace to the humble.' Therefore submit to God. Resist the devil and he will flee from you. Draw near to God and He will draw near to you. Cleanse your hands, you sinners; and purify your

hearts, you double-minded. Lament and mourn and weep! Let your laughter be turned to mourning and your joy to gloom. Humble yourselves in the sight of the Lord, and He will lift you up.

—*James 4:4–10*

The Mystery of God's Will

*Having made known to us the mystery of His will,
according to His good pleasure which He purposed in
Himself*

—Ephesians 1:9

SCRIPTURE: *Ephesians 1*

Paul relates the blessings with which God has blessed us
in the heavenly places, according to the riches of His grace,
and then declares the mystery of His will which He has made
known to us "in all wisdom and prudence" (Ephesians 1:8).
God reveals His purposes by a gradual progression, just as
Jesus gradually unfolded His truths to His disciples. On the
eve of His crucifixion, He said to them, "I still have many
things to say to you, but you cannot bear them now" (John
16:12). The Spirit of Truth would guide them into all the
truth, and so it is with the mystery of God's will.

What a vast vision is here disclosed to view! The universe
is to be made anew in Christ. All things in the heavens and
on the earth are to be reunited under His headship. All the
dispensations, or stages of God's revelations over the ages,
have been leading up to this great day. All the dealings of God
which have characterized the various ages will receive their
culmination in that age, and in this sense it will be "the fullness of the times."

Christ will be the uniting bond of all things. In Him, through Him, and for Him were all things created (Colossians 1:16). "For it pleased the Father that in Him all the fullness should dwell, and by Him to reconcile all things to Himself, by Him, whether things on earth or things in heaven, having made peace through the blood of His cross" (Colossians 1:19–20).

✣ FAITH IN GOD ✣

Faith in God stands in contrast to simple belief, which consists of an opinion held in good "faith" without necessarily having any proof. The object of Abraham's faith was not God's promise; his faith rested on God Himself (Romans 4:17, 20–21).

As we have been seeing throughout our reflections, God is absolutely sovereign over all events on earth. Yet we have also seen that there is an element of human free will, an opportunity for men and women to voluntarily submit themselves to the will and commands of God. This raises the question that most Christians ask from time to time: What is God's will in this matter or that situation? At first glance, this might be the sense one imparts to the term "the mystery of God's will," but it is not the sense the Scriptures have in mind.

Paul refers to the mystery of God's will in reference to God's overall plan of redemption for mankind, a plan He instituted "before the foundation of the world, that we should be holy and without blame before Him in love" (Ephesians 1:4), a plan to pay for the sins of repentant men and women through the sinless sacrifice of His Son. He prophesied this event on the very day when Adam sinned (Genesis 3:15), and He brought it to fruition on the cross. This mystery is that those who accept God's gift of grace "have obtained an inheritance, being predestined according to the purpose of Him who works all things according to the counsel of His will" (Ephesians 1:11). This is the eternal life that becomes the inheritance of all who submit to Christ, an eternal gift that was predestined before the foundations of the earth and that can never be taken away.

The question of understanding God's will in day-to-day matters for each believer is not a mystery. The Bible clearly reveals what is entailed in understanding the will of God in our daily lives, as we have seen numerous times under the subject of submission and obedience. Paul sums it up neatly in Romans: "I beseech you therefore, brethren, by the mercies of God, that you present your bodies a living sacrifice, holy, acceptable to God, which is your reasonable service. And do not be conformed to this world, but be transformed by the renewing of your mind, that you may prove what is that good and acceptable and perfect will of God" (Romans

12:1–2). A believer comes to understand the will of God in his life by renewing his mind, and this is done by regular disciplines of Bible study, prayer, meditation, and fellowship with other believers. As a believer's mind is renewed, he begins to develop the habits of thinking as God thinks, and in this sense a believer comes to know the mind of God (Romans 8:26–27).

The Mystery of God's Will

Union in Christ

The devil, who deceived them, was cast into the lake of fire and brimstone where the beast and the false prophet are. And they will be tormented day and night forever and ever.

—Revelation 20:10

SCRIPTURE: *Luke 16*

The first stage of the union between Christ and His church will take place at the beginning of the millennial reign of Christ, at the time when the mystery of God will be finished. The destruction of antichrist and his associates, the deliverance of the Jews from their oppressors, and the binding and removal of Satan will be followed by Messiah's reign of righteousness and peace. But this itself will be only a prelude to the complete fulfillment of the mystery of God's will in Christ. The consummation of all will take place in the age to follow, when there will be no discord in the new heavens and earth, as all things will be joyfully submitting to the will of God.

We must observe that this union of all things in Christ extends to things in the heavens and things on the earth, but

CLASSIC REFLECTIONS *on* SCRIPTURE

it is not said to embrace things "under the earth," the third sphere mentioned in Philippians 2:10. The notion that those who die in their sins will one day have another opportunity to receive salvation is frequently contradicted in Scripture, and it cannot find any support in Ephesians 1:10: "That . . . He might gather together in one all things in Christ, both which are in heaven and which are on earth." This passage does not offer any warrant for any person to presume upon the mercy of God, expecting to be reconciled with Him in eternity despite refusing to repent in this life. God's pardoning grace is offered freely to all men now by accepting His terms of grace and redemption through the death of His Son.

๛ HELL ๛

The New Testament word translated *hell* is *geenna*, drawn from the Hebrew *Gê-Hinnom* (the valley of Tophet) and a corresponding Aramaic word. It is found twelve times in the New Testament, and in every instance it is uttered by the Lord Himself. In Matthew 18:8, Jesus speaks of hell as "everlasting fire." Mark 9:43–47 parallels the Matthew passage and adds the descriptions "their worm does not die" and "the fire is not quenched."

There is a notion that has recently regained a foothold within the Christian church, claiming that people who reject Christ in this life will have another opportunity in eternity to accept His free gift of salvation. This notion is a lie. It is not a new concept; the same idea was espoused by false teachers, such as Origen, within the early church. Throughout the history of the church, such false teachers have arisen who seduce believers into error by claiming that a loving God could never condemn a human being to eternal suffering simply because he refused to accept God's free gift of salvation.

In the Scriptures, God makes it abundantly clear that there is a season of grace available to all men, a time when any individual may repent of his sins and submit himself to the atoning sacrifice of Christ. That season of grace does not last forever, but the results of each person's choice *do* last forever. The Bible is clear that the suffering of hell is eternal, not a temporary condition (Revelation 14:11; 20:10). Hell consists of an eternal separation from God, and there is no opportunity for a person to be accepted into God's presence once he has finally rejected the only means of salvation through Christ. Jesus made this clear when He spoke in Luke 16 about Lazarus the beggar and a certain rich man who rejected salvation. That rich man begged Abraham to send Lazarus to him to ease his torment, but Abraham replied, "Between us and you there is a great gulf fixed, so that those who want to pass from here to you cannot, nor can those from there pass to us" (Luke 16:26).

The time of grace is now! Today is the day of God's free gift of salvation; tomorrow may well be too late. "Beware, brethren, lest there be in any of you an evil heart of unbelief in departing from the living God; but exhort one another daily, while it is called 'Today,' lest any of you be hardened through the deceitfulness of sin. For we have become partakers of Christ if we hold the beginning of our confidence steadfast to the end, while it is said: 'Today, if you will hear His voice, do not harden your hearts as in the rebellion'" (Hebrews 3:12–15).

The Completion of the Mysteries

But in the days of the sounding of the seventh angel, when he is about to sound, the mystery of God would be finished, as He declared to His servants the prophets.

—Revelation 10:7

SCRIPTURE: *Philippians 2*

At the time of God's judgment, "the mystery of God would be finished, as He declared to His servants the prophets" (Revelation 10:7)—a mystery hidden in past ages but made known to those who have already bowed in submission to the Son of God. The mystery is said to be finished at the time when the seventh angel of Revelation sounds his trumpet, because all the prophecies will be fulfilled concerning this age and the intervention of God at its close. As in the pouring out of the vials, the wrath of God is "complete" (Revelation 15:1), so the mystery of God will be finished in the overthrow of unrighteousness and the establishment of the kingdom of righteousness. The good tidings proclaim the triumph of Christ in the deliverance of the groaning creation and the beginning of His reign of peace.

Now, when the church is complete and has been caught up to meet the Lord at the commencement of His eternal reign, it will come forth with Him in the revelation of His glory to the world. This will be the shining forth of His presence with His saints, "when He comes, in that Day, to be glorified in His saints and to be admired among all those who believe" (2 Thessalonians 1:10). The world has refused to acknowledge Him, but it will be compelled to recognize His deity, and will witness the union of the church with its Redeemer. That mystery of God will be fully revealed.

ꙮ 2 *THESSALONIANS 1:10* ꙮ

saints . . . all those who believe: The two expressions, "saints" and "all those who believe," might describe the whole number of the redeemed who are to accompany the Lord at His coming; i.e., all who are Christ's, whether of this age or of the last (1 Corinthians 15:23). Or "saints" might refer to the redeemed of former ages, and "all those who believe" might refer to "the church, which is His body" (Ephesians 1:22–23).

God's entire creation was subjected to death and suffering on the day when Adam sinned, though not willingly so. For who would voluntarily subject himself to death, we might ask, voluntarily undergoing decay and suffering and hardship? Yet the sad fact is that such is precisely what Adam did, for he knew in advance that disobedience to God would result in death (Genesis 2:17). And ever since that day, "the whole creation groans and labors with birth pangs together" (Romans 8:22). The groaning is creation's response to suffering and death, inflicted upon it by our disobedience—but the birth pangs are the anticipation of the full revelation of God's mystery of redemption and grace, a revelation that cannot be thwarted.

But this revelation comes at a great cost, not to us but to God Himself. For the true answer to the question—who would voluntarily submit to death and suffering?—is found in Christ. He was eternally present with the Father and an inseparable person of the Godhead, yet He chose willingly to leave eternity and enter our world in the form of a man, specifically for the purpose of submitting Himself to death. This in itself is a deep mystery, how He who is Life could make Himself subject to death, yet He did so because of God's great love for those who were created in His image.

The full revelation of this mystery must wait until eternity, but in this world we still gain a small glimpse of God's immeasurable grace. He takes those who are hopelessly bound in sin and death and transforms us into the likeness of His Son, the spotless Lamb of God. We participate in this process by transforming our minds (Romans 12:1–2), learning to think as God thinks. As Paul stated, "Let this mind be in you which was also in Christ Jesus, who, being in the form of God, did not consider it robbery to be equal with God, but made Himself of no reputation, taking the form of a bond-servant, and coming in the likeness of men. And being found in appearance as a man, He humbled Himself and became obedient to the point of death, even the death of the cross" (Philippians 2:5–8).

For Further Study

Mystery (*mystērion*)

Matthew 13:11
Mark 4:11
Luke 8:10
Romans 11:25; 16:25
1 Corinthians 2:7; 4:1; 13:2; 14:2; 15:51
Ephesians 1:9; 3:3, 4, 9; 5:32; 6:19
Colossians 1:26, 27; 2:2; 4:3
2 Thessalonians 2:7
1 Timothy 3:9, 16
Revelation 1:20; 10:7; 17:5, 7

Faith (*pistis*)

Matthew 8:10; 9:2, 22, 29; 15:28; 17:20; 21:21; 23:23
Mark 2:5; 4:40; 5:34; 10:52; 11:22
Luke 5:20; 7:9, 50; 8:25, 48; 17:5, 6, 19; 18:8, 42; 22:32
Acts 3:16; 6:5, 7, 8; 11:24; 13:8; 14:9, 22, 27; 15:9; 16:5; 20:21; 24:24; 26:18
Romans 1:5, 8, 12, 17; 3:3, 22, 25–28, 30, 31; 4:5, 9, 11–14, 16, 19, 20; 5:1, 2; 9:30, 32; 10:6, 8, 17; 12:3, 6; 14:1, 22, 23, 26
1 Corinthians 2:5; 12:9; 13:2, 13; 15:14, 17; 16:13
2 Corinthians 1:24; 4:13; 5:7; 8:7; 10:15; 13:5
Galatians 1:23; 2:16, 20; 3:2, 5, 7–9, 11–14, 22–26; 5:5, 6, 22; 6:10
Ephesians 1:15; 2:8; 3:12, 17; 4:5, 13; 6:16, 23
Philippians 1:25, 27; 2:17; 3:9
Colossians 1:4, 23; 2:5, 7, 12
1 Thessalonians 1:3, 8; 3:2, 5–7, 10; 5:8
2 Thessalonians 1:3, 4, 11; 3:2
1 Timothy 1:2, 4, 5, 14, 19; 2:7, 15; 3:9, 13; 4:1, 6, 12; 5:8, 12; 6:10–12, 21
2 Timothy 1:5, 13; 2:18, 22; 3:8, 10, 15; 4:7

Titus 1:1, 4, 13; 2:2; 3:15
Philemon 1:5, 6
Hebrews 4:2; 6:1, 12; 10:22, 38, 39; 11:1, 3–9, 11, 13, 17, 20–24, 27–31, 33; 12:2; 13:7
James 1:3, 6; 2:1, 5, 14, 17, 18, 20, 22, 24, 26; 5:15
1 Peter 1:5, 7, 9, 21; 5:9
2 Peter 1:1, 5
1 John 5:4
Jude 1:3, 20
Revelation 2:13, 19; 13:10; 14:12

Resurrection (*anastasis*)

Matthew 22:23, 28, 30, 31
Mark 12:18, 23
Luke 2:34; 14:14; 20:27, 33, 35, 36
John 5:29; 11:24, 25
Acts 1:22; 2:31; 4:2, 33; 17:18, 32; 23:6, 8; 24:15, 21; 26:23
Romans 1:4; 6:5
1 Corinthians 15:12, 13, 21, 42
Philippians 3:10
2 Timothy 2:18
Hebrews 6:2; 11:35
1 Peter 1:3; 3:21
Revelation 20:5, 6

The Four

Women of

Revelation

Section Contents

Four Women of Revelation

Jezebel

    Jezebel and Ahab

Babylon

    Babylon and the Beast

A Woman Clothed with the Sun

    The Woman and the Male Child

    The Woman and the Dragon

The Bride, the Lamb's Wife

    Concerning Christ and the Church

    The City's Temple

    The River and the Tree

    The Lamb and the Stone

For Further Study

The Four Women of Revelation

Nevertheless I have a few things against you, because you allow that woman Jezebel, who calls herself a prophetess, to teach and seduce My servants to commit sexual immorality and eat things sacrificed to idols.

—Revelation 2:20

SCRIPTURE: *Revelation 2*

The book of Revelation describes four women who will play some role during the last days: Jezebel, Babylon, a woman clothed with the sun, and the bride of the Lamb. Two of these women (Jezebel, Babylon) symbolize agencies that spread corruption throughout the earth, while the other two symbolize the two great communities which God has formed to bear witness for Him and to act as His instruments of government in the ages that are to come. We will look at each of these women in this section.

Thyatira Trade Guilds

Some background will be helpful concerning the trade guilds located in the city of Thyatira. Thyatira was situated northeast of Smyrna, in a fertile valley in the Province of Asia, an area which offered its inhabitants many commercial advantages.

The citizens were formed into several trade guilds, and one's worldly success was largely determined by membership in them. Guild feasts were held at appointed times, and the proceedings on these occasions were characterized by the utmost licentiousness. The guilds themselves were organized in accordance with which pagan god a person worshiped, and the guild feasts included a sacrifice to that particular god, followed by a meal from the offerings. Moreover, one could not be a member of one of these guilds without also being a worshiper of the guild's god. Yet at the same time, a businessman or merchant who refused to join a guild was held in contempt and viewed with suspicion as being an enemy of mankind.

ᦸ *IDOL* ᦸ

The Hebrew word used in the Old Testament for *idol* denotes *vanity*, or *thing of naught*. Hence what represented a deity to the gentiles was to Paul a "vain thing." Jeremiah calls the idol a "scarecrow."

The ancient city of Thyatira was a prosperous commercial center, particularly noted for its trade in indigo and its skill in dying fabrics. As with many other prosperous cities, commerce and business was a top priority, and commercial success was a driving force in the lives of its citizens. Trade guilds were a way of ensuring ongoing success to the city, and there were guilds for practically every type of trade; potters, bakers, slave-traders, and every aspect of garment manufacturing were connected with one or another of those guilds. Anyone who wanted to advance in a career would be expected to join at least one of these guilds, as they were sources of what we today refer to as "networking."

The fact is things have not changed much since ancient times. In modern Western societies, climbing the career ladder is still a high priority, and networking with other career-minded people is part of that process. Success in the business world in itself is not evil, nor is it ungodly to network with others for mutual financial benefit. The problem comes when the goal of success supplants the higher priority of godliness, and this can be a very subtle process that leads a Christian to make small compromises that seem innocuous at the time.

The trade guilds of Thyatira pressured their members to participate in a variety of ungodly practices, things that might not seem to have direct parallels to business dealings of modern times. But any compromise with holiness is a step away from God and toward wickedness, and even the smallest step in that direction can be damaging to one's relationship with God. Paul warned of the dangers of being unequally yoked within marriage, and that principle applies in business dealings as well.

Do not be unequally yoked together with unbelievers. For what fellowship has righteousness with lawlessness? And what communion has light with darkness? And what accord has Christ with Belial? Or what part has a believer with an unbeliever? And what agreement has the temple of God with idols? For you are the temple of the living God. As God has said: "I will dwell in them and walk among them. I will be their God, and they shall be My people." Therefore "Come out from among them and be separate, says the Lord. Do not touch what is unclean, and I will receive you."

—*2 Corinthians 6:14–17*

Jezebel

For men will be lovers of themselves, lovers of money, boasters, proud, blasphemers, disobedient to parents, unthankful, unholy, unloving, unforgiving, slanderers, without self-control, brutal, despisers of good, traitors, headstrong, haughty, lovers of pleasure rather than lovers of God, having a form of godliness but denying its power. And from such people turn away!

—2 Timothy 3:2–5

SCRIPTURE: *2 Timothy 3*

The first of the four women of Revelation is described in the letter to the church in Thyatira (Revelation 2:18–29). She was corrupting the Lord's servants in that city, and the Lord rebuked the church there for allowing her presence and influence. He stated, "I have a few things against you, because you allow that woman Jezebel, who calls herself a prophetess, to teach and seduce My servants to commit sexual immorality and eat things sacrificed to idols" (v. 20).

The woman called Jezebel was posing as a prophetess; in today's thinking, she would have been seen as the advocate of broad-mindedness and enlightenment. She would easily seduce the careless believer to go in for membership of a guild (see the introduction to this section), or to return to it if it had been abandoned at the time of salvation. The advantages would be great, she would suggest: ridicule and persecution would be avoided, prosperity in business would be practically ensured, and personal prestige in the city would be enhanced. And why not bring a healthy influence into society by joining the guild? These and other arguments, with which Christians are so familiar today, would be used to entice believers from their faithfulness to Christ.

This woman introduced doctrines into the church by which she lured some of the believers to partake in the licentious and idolatrous practices referred to—sexual immorality and eating foods sacrificed to idols (both hallmarks of the guilds). Here, then, in the early days of church history, lawlessness became rife and immorality was practiced under the garb of the Christian faith, "having a form of godliness but denying its power" (2 Timothy 3:5).

ᔟ 2 TIMOTHY 3:5 ᔟ

from such people turn away: This phrase might be better translated "from these also turn away." We are commanded to turn away from the openly sinful characters listed in the previous verses, but also to turn away from those who have a form of godliness but deny its power. These are called out because their outward form of religion might make an appeal for a certain amount of fellowship. This, however, is forbidden equally with all those listed previously in the passage.

In 2 Timothy 3, Paul painted a grim picture of what society would be like "in the last days" (v. 1). Here are some of the qualities that will characterize society in the end times:

- ✥ lovers of self
- ✥ lovers of money
- ✥ boastful
- ✥ blasphemous
- ✥ disobedient to authority
- ✥ unthankful
- ✥ unforgiving
- ✥ having no self-control
- ✥ traitors
- ✥ lovers of pleasure

Of course, this list could be seen as merely a small picture of our fallen human nature, as every descendant of Adam has the capacity—indeed, the tendency—to pursue any and all of these forms of ungodliness. Yet an honest assessment of modern culture cannot fail to notice that this description is very apt to our world today. The culture of self-esteem or self-love, to choose just the first item in the list, trains our children from an early age to love themselves rather than to love others and to love God. In the context of Jezebel and the trade guilds of Thyatira, we can also see the widespread tendency in our culture to love money more than godliness.

This woman has direct parallels in today's world. One of the great fears of our age is to be called "closed-minded," to be accused of being bigoted against others who might think differently. But God's Word does not command us to be "open-minded," to pretend that false beliefs concerning God and eternity might actually be true and valid for another person. On the contrary, Paul commanded his readers to turn away from people who espouse lies: "From such people turn away!" (2 Timothy 3:5). Our modern culture of "open-mindedness" is merely a new disguise for the old sin of rejecting God's truth. Such people today are "always learning and never able to come to the knowledge of the truth" (2 Timothy 3:7). From such, God's people should turn away.

Jezebel and Ahab

Nevertheless I have a few things against you, because you allow that woman Jezebel, who calls herself a prophetess, to teach and seduce My servants to commit sexual immorality and eat things sacrificed to idols.

—Revelation 2:20

SCRIPTURE: *1 Kings 19*

The name *Jezebel* evokes Old Testament connections, urging us to look back to 1 Kings. The Jezebel found in the Old Testament was the daughter of Ethbaal, a Sidonian. Her father was priest to Astarte, the vile goddess of the Syrians and a false religion practiced in Babylon. Jezebel married King Ahab, so as queen she introduced foreign practices into Israel. The story of her pollution of the nation is well known, how she slaughtered the prophets of God and substituted the prophets of Baal. Through her efforts and influence, Ahab "did evil in the sight of the LORD, more than all who were before him" (1 Kings 16:30).

The worship of Astarte replaced that of Jehovah. Jezebel's baneful influence continued during the reigns of her two sons, Ahaziah and Jehoram, and it extended to the tribe of Judah through the marriage of her daughter to the son of Jehoshaphat, king of Judah. We can safely assume that worship of false gods was becoming evident in the church of

Thyatira, as the Lord was drawing a distinct parallel between the woman of Thyatira and the wife of Ahab.

What took place in the narrower sphere of Thyatira continues to threaten the church today. We cannot definitely say whether those who were guilty of yielding to Jezebel's seductions in Thyatira actually repented of their deeds, or whether the Lord's threat was carried out. But the force of the Lord's warning is just as relevant to us today: "I will kill her children with death, and all the churches shall know that I am He who searches the minds and hearts. And I will give to each one of you according to your works" (Revelation 2:23).

✧ *IDOL* ✧

The Greek word translated *idol* refers to "a phantom or likeness" (from a root word meaning "an appearance; that which is seen"). It can also mean "an idea or fancy." It is used in the New Testament to refer to an idol, an image to represent a false god.

Ahab was king over Israel during the period of the divided kingdom, when the Jews were separated into the nations of Israel and Judah. He blatantly disregarded the Lord's command not to marry women from foreign nations (Exodus

34:16; 1 Kings 11:2), and Jezebel brought all her pagan idolatries with her into Israel. He might have intended the marriage as a political expedient, hoping to establish some sort of international treaty with the nation of Sidon as Solomon had done years earlier (1 Kings 11:5), but the end results were the same as Solomon's: his idolatrous wife led him into further sin, and that sin spread to the people of God—not only in Israel but into Judah as well.

Human nature tends to view God as some sort of killjoy, a despotic and mean-spirited ruler who commands His people to refrain from having fun. This, of course, is a foolish way of thinking, like a spoiled child who becomes angry when told to eat his vegetables. When God commands His people to do or to refrain from some behavior, it is for good reason, and it is always for our benefit. Jezebel and Ahab disregarded the Word of God and insisted upon doing things their own way, intent upon fulfilling their own priorities rather than submitting to God's will.

God commended His people in the letters to the churches (Revelation 2 and 3) for various acts of obedience and faithfulness, but He also made it clear that He does not tolerate compromise with the world's values. This woman who lived in Thyatira wanted to change the Word of God in order to accommodate the ways of the world, teaching others that scriptural doctrines on sexual purity did not apply to the church any longer, urging believers to be no different from the world around them; and the Lord's response to this was dramatic: "I will kill her children with death" (Revelation 2:23).

God insists that His children obey His Word, yet He is also faithful to reward obedience and to discipline disobedience. "All the churches shall know that I am He who searches the minds and hearts. And I will give to each one of you according to your works" (2:23).

Babylon

"Come, I will show you the judgment of the great harlot who sits on many waters, with whom the kings of the earth committed fornication, and the inhabitants of the earth were made drunk with the wine of her fornication."

—Revelation 17:1–2

SCRIPTURE: *Revelation 17*

The second of the evil women described in Revelation is found in chapter 17. The apostle John was carried away in the spirit into a wilderness, a place that suggests destitution, symbolizing a condition barren of all that is fruitful for God and void of that which could delight His eye. (This presents a striking contrast, as we shall see, to the place from which the apostle was afterwards called to see the bride of the Lamb.)

He now sees a woman "sitting on a scarlet beast which was full of names of blasphemy, having seven heads and ten horns. The woman was arrayed in purple and scarlet, and adorned with gold and precious stones and pearls, having in her hand a golden cup full of abominations and the filthiness of her fornication. And on her forehead a name was written: MYSTERY, BABYLON THE GREAT, THE MOTHER OF HARLOTS AND OF THE ABOMINATIONS OF THE EARTH" (Revelation 17:3–5).

The woman's name, *Babylon the Great*, connects her with the ancient city of Babylon. But notice that the word

Mystery is added to the title. This implies that the name has a spiritual significance, that facts relating to the woman have something more than a mere geographical and historical connection with the city of Babylon. A *mystery* in Scripture does not refer to something obscure and "mysterious," as we have already considered; rather, it refers to facts the reader is intended to understand—truths that help him shape his conduct according to the will of God. A *mystery* lies outside the comprehension of the natural mind, for "the natural man does not receive the things of the Spirit of God . . . because they are spiritually discerned" (1 Corinthians 2:14).

⁓ ABOMINATION ⁓

The Greek word translated *abomination* denotes an "object of disgust." This word is used to describe the image to be set up by antichrist (Matthew 24:15). It refers to things that are highly esteemed by men in spite of their real character in the sight of God (Luke 16:15). The constant association with idolatry suggests that what is highly esteemed among men constitutes an idol in the human heart.

The last phrase of the woman's title, "the Mother of Harlots and of the Abominations of the Earth," suggests that Babylon is the source of unholy unions, unequal yoking between the people of God and the world, for such associations are described in Scripture as spiritual fornication

(Jeremiah 3:6, 8, 9; Ezekiel 16:32). The woman also represents all forms of idolatry in the world, for anything that men worship apart from God is an abomination. The language also suggests the immorality and unchaste behavior that accompanies idolatry.

Many theories abound concerning the mystery of Babylon that the Lord addresses in the book of Revelation, but the fact is that the entire mystery has yet to be fully revealed. It will become more clear as the time of God's final judgment draws near on earth; in the meantime, we can learn more of God's will from the picture of the woman called Babylon, principles that are pertinent to God's people in all generations. She is a picture of the world's values embodying the traits of those who oppose the lordship of Christ—in short, exactly what God's people should *not* be.

The description of Babylon focuses to a large degree on sexual matters, as she is "the great harlot . . . with whom the kings of the earth committed fornication" (Revelation 17:1, 2). This issue certainly has application in the literal sense, as sexual immorality is an abomination in the eyes of God, but the sexual abominations of Babylon can also be broadened into the area of spiritual adultery, and this is perhaps the more pertinent application in the church today. Spiritual adultery is the intermingling of false doctrines with the truth of Scripture, a tendency that is widespread in the church. The Lord condemned spiritual adultery in Israel and Judah: "Have you seen what backsliding Israel has done? She has gone up on every high mountain and under every green tree, and there played the harlot.... So it came to pass, through her casual harlotry, that [Judah] defiled the land and committed adultery with stones and trees" (Jeremiah 3:6, 9). The Word of God is complete in itself, and any attempt to add in the world's teachings is an abomination in God's eyes.

Babylon and the Beast

And I saw a woman sitting on a scarlet beast which was full of names of blasphemy, having seven heads and ten horns. The woman was arrayed in purple and scarlet, and adorned with gold and precious stones and pearls, having in her hand a golden cup full of abominations and the filthiness of her fornication.

—Revelation 17:3–4

SCRIPTURE: *Daniel 7*

The woman called Babylon is seen sitting on a scarlet-colored, seven-headed, ten-horned beast. The beast is indicated as the head of the ten-kingdom league of nations. A comparison of Revelation 17 with Revelation 13 and Daniel 7 shows that the term "beast" is symbolic of a monarch and his dominion (Daniel 7:17, 23). The woman, by contrast, will one day occupy a position of religious and political domination over the nations. She rides the beast, governing the political power, and she also "sits on many waters," which are interpreted as "peoples, multitudes, nations, and tongues" (Revelation 17:1, 15). That is to say, besides controlling the ten-kingdom league with its rulers, she exercises her influence over the masses of the people.

John saw the woman "drunk with the blood of the saints and with the blood of the martyrs of Jesus" (Revelation 17:6). Everything that is represented by Babylon is guilty of the slaughter of saints of God. The same spirit that leads men to the abominations of idolatry likewise instigates them to the persecution of His people. The political rulers of the earth will be intoxicated by the wine of the woman's abominations, lured by her pomp and grandeur, while she herself will be intoxicated by the blood of the true followers of Christ.

Her doom, however, is sealed. Her destruction is destined to take place at the hands of the very political leaders who had supported her. The change in the situation is dramatic. "And the ten horns that you saw, they and the beast [not "the ten horns which you saw *on* the beast," as in NKJV] will hate the whore; they will make her desolate and naked; they will devour her flesh and burn her up with fire" (Revelation 17:16, NRSV).

᪽ BEAST ᪽

The Greek word here translated *beast* almost invariably denotes "a wild beast," as opposed to another word used in Scripture that simply denotes "an animal." This word is used in Revelation for the two anti-Christian rulers who are destined to control the affairs of the nations with satanic power in the closing period of the present era.

How this will actually transpire is made clear in Revelation 13. The two beasts, the confederate world rulers, will establish a universal religion that goes along with their universal political dominion. Its creed will be simple but absolute: the world ruler must be acknowledged as God, and refusal to do so will be punished by death.

> And he deceives those who dwell on the earth by those signs which he was granted to do in the sight of the beast, telling those who dwell on the earth to make an image to the beast who was wounded by the sword and lived. He was granted power to give breath to the image of the beast, that the image of the beast should both speak and cause as many as would not worship the image of the beast to be killed.
>
> —*Revelation 13:14–15*

The power at the disposal of these two world rulers will be sufficient to enforce this worship, and every other religion must be crushed.

As already stated, the mystery of Babylon has not yet been fully revealed, and a complete understanding of these matters will come only in the time of the last things as described in Revelation and Daniel. Yet we can still glean some important glimpses of the things that are to come in the last days, particularly in what those times will be like on earth.

These grim days will see worldwide persecution of the followers of Christ. The Scripture further suggests that this persecution will be severe, to the point that the servants of the evil one will become "drunk" with the blood of the saints. But believers must not lose heart and become fearful of the future, for all these things are under our Father's absolute control; indeed, they are all part of His plan, and as such they will be for the glory of God and perfection of His children. The world's values represented by the whore of Babylon will be destroyed and devoured by the very beast that she rides (Revelation 17:16), and in the end the wicked one and all his servants will be cast into the lake of fire forever (19:19–21). "For God has put it into their hearts to fulfill His purpose, to be of one mind, and to give their kingdom to the beast, until the words of God are fulfilled" (17:17).

A Woman Clothed with the Sun

Now a great sign appeared in heaven: a woman clothed with the sun, with the moon under her feet, and on her head a garland of twelve stars.

—Revelation 12:1

SCRIPTURE: *Revelation 12*

We are now to consider the two other women depicted in Revelation, whose characters are entirely different from the two women whom we have already considered. The first is described in Revelation 12. This chapter really has its beginning in the last verse of chapter 11: "Then the temple of God was opened in heaven, and the ark of His covenant was seen in His temple. And there were lightnings, noises, thunderings, an earthquake, and great hail" (v. 19). These mentions of the temple and the ark of the covenant indicate that what follows in chapter 12 has to do with the nation of Israel. It is in this context that chapters 12 through 14 are to be taken together, and carry us through affairs connected with Israel from the time of the birth of Christ till the end of the Great Tribulation and the overthrow of antichrist by the Son of Man.

The apostle John was shown a great sign in heaven, "a woman clothed with the sun, with the moon under her feet, and on her head a garland of twelve stars" (Revelation 12:1). The fact that she is arrayed with the sun possibly points to Israel being under the protecting power of God, which is directly set forth later in the chapter. The fact that the moon (an emblem of secondary authority) is seen under her feet indicates that the power she might have exercised under God has gone from her, and that she is in a position of subjection to her foes. At the same time, there is a suggestion that she will yet be given supreme authority on the earth.

The first mention in the Bible of the sun, moon, and stars is in connection with the government of the earth (Genesis 1:16). The crown of twelve stars indicates the glory of the worldwide authority that God has determined for His chosen nation of Israel. He has said, "I will make . . . the outcast a strong nation; so the LORD will reign over them in Mount Zion from now on, even forever. And you, O tower of the flock, the stronghold of the daughter of Zion, to you shall it come, even the former dominion shall come, the kingdom of the daughter of Jerusalem" (Micah 4:7–8).

Using the analogy of childbirth, Isaiah uttered a prediction concerning Israel that provides a key to Revelation 12. The prophet foretold that the historical order would be the reverse of the natural process of birth, in connection with the birth of Christ and the future time of the Great Tribulation. Of Israel, he says, "Before she was in labor, she gave birth; before her pain came, she delivered a male child. Who has heard such a thing? Who has seen such things?" (Isaiah 66:7–8). Then Isaiah goes on to say that a remnant of the nation will be preserved through the time of trouble and brought into millennial glory: "'Shall the earth be made to give birth in one day? Or shall a nation be born at once? For as soon as Zion was in labor, she gave birth to her children. Shall I bring to the time of birth, and not cause delivery?' says the LORD. 'Shall I who cause delivery shut up the womb?' says your God" (Isaiah 66:8–9).

↝ DECEIVE ↝

The Greek word translated *deceive* can be used in the passive form to mean "go astray, wander." In Revelation 12, however, it is used in the active form, meaning "to deceive by leading into error, to seduce, to lead astray." In Revelation 12:9, it is used as a title of the Devil, "the Deceiver," "the deceiving one." Often it has the sense of "deceiving oneself" (1 Corinthians 6:9; 15:33).

The Lord thus assures His people Israel that they shall be completely and suddenly delivered from their relentless foes and that a remnant shall be saved (although the nation itself will be decimated). The timeframe of this is during the Millennium, which is clear from the joyous predictions that follow: "Rejoice with Jerusalem, and be glad with her, all you who love her; rejoice for joy with her, all you who mourn for her. . . . For thus says the LORD: 'Behold, I will extend peace to her like a river, and the glory of the Gentiles like a flowing stream. . . . As one whom his mother comforts, so I will comfort you; and you shall be comforted in Jerusalem, . . . The hand of the LORD shall be known to His servants, and His indignation to His enemies" (Isaiah 66:10, 12–14).

The nation of Israel came under God's discipline when the people rejected the Messiah and nailed Him to the cross. But God's discipline will not remain indefinitely, and the day is coming when the descendants of Abraham will once again receive a special blessing from God as His chosen people. God has promised repeatedly that the Jewish people will remain His chosen nation, and His promises never fail. During times of horrible persecution, the people of Israel might say, "The LORD has forsaken me, and my Lord has forgotten me," but God will answer, "Can a woman forget her nursing child, and not have compassion on the son of her womb? Surely they may forget, yet I will not forget you. See, I have inscribed you on the palms of My hands; your walls are continually before Me" (Isaiah 49:14–16).

Yet the fact remains that God's discipline can be painful for those who have refused to obey His Word. During such times, a believer can slip into despair, thinking that God has abandoned him; or bitterness and resentment can grow, leading the believer even farther from the repentance and submission that God is trying to cultivate. For that is the purpose behind all discipline: to perfect a Christian's character, making him more like Christ and leading him to a deeper trusting obedience to God's Word. As James reminds us, "My brethren, count it all joy when you fall into various trials, knowing that the testing of your faith produces patience. But let patience have its perfect work, that you may be perfect and complete, lacking nothing" (James 1:2–4).

When we undergo times of trial, our first response should be to examine our lives in light of God's Word to see if there is any area of disobedience that needs to be corrected. The writer of Hebrews states it this way:

> And you have forgotten the exhortation which speaks to you as to sons: "My son, do not despise the chastening of the LORD, nor be discouraged when you are rebuked by Him; for whom the Lord loves He chastens, and scourges every son whom He receives." If you endure chastening, God deals with you as with sons; for what son is there whom a father does not chasten? . . . Now no chastening seems to be joyful for the present, but painful; nevertheless, afterward it yields the peaceable fruit of righteousness to those who have been trained by it. Therefore strengthen the hands which hang down, and the feeble knees, and make straight paths for your feet, so that what is lame may not be dislocated, but rather be healed.

—*Hebrews 12:5–7, 11–13*

The Woman and the Male Child

Now when the dragon saw that he had been cast to the earth, he persecuted the woman who gave birth to the male Child.

—Revelation 12:13

SCRIPTURE: *Isaiah 9*

One cannot consider the depictions of the four women in Revelation without also looking closely at the absolutely essential figure of the "male Child" mentioned in Revelation 12:5. Isaiah foretold that the nation of Israel would give birth to the One who would break the yoke of Israel's enemies and who would be its Deliverer, saying, "For unto us a Child is born, unto us a Son is given; and the government will be upon His shoulder. And His name will be called Wonderful, Counselor, Mighty God, Everlasting Father, Prince of Peace. Of the increase of His government and peace there will be no end, upon the throne of David and over His kingdom, to order it and establish it with judgment and justice from that time forward, even forever. The zeal of the Lord of hosts will perform this" (Isaiah 9:6–7).

Micah spoke of the same events. He specified the tribe into which the male Child would be born and the place of

His birth: "'But you, Bethlehem Ephrathah, though you are little among the thousands of Judah, yet out of you shall come forth to Me the One to be Ruler in Israel, whose goings forth are from of old, from everlasting.' Therefore He shall give them up, until the time that she who is in labor has given birth; then the remnant of His brethren shall return to the children of Israel" (Micah 5:2–3).

⤳ 2 TIMOTHY 1:9 ⤳

according to His own purpose and grace: The word *own* bears a special stress, signifying that God's purpose sprang solely from His good will and love and not from anything external to Himself.

The woman whom John sees in Revelation 12 is Israel, and her male Child is Christ. The woman "bore a male Child" (Revelation 12:5) when Christ was born in Bethlehem—long before the time of her travail, for that is yet to take place at the close of the present age. It is Christ who shall break Israel's enemies with a rod of iron. "I will declare the decree: The LORD has said to Me, 'You are My Son, today I have begotten You. Ask of Me, and I will give You the nations for Your inheritance, and the ends of the earth for Your possession. You shall break them with a rod of iron; You shall dash them to pieces like a potter's vessel'" (Psalm 2:7–9). The description of Him as a "male Child" in Revelation 12 suggests His perfect humanity, because of which the Father "has given Him authority to execute judgment" (John 5:27).

All of earth's history is centered upon the return of Christ. This future event was foreordained before the foundations of the earth were even laid (Ephesians 1:4; 2 Timothy 1:9; 1 Peter 1:20), and God spoke of the coming Redeemer on the very day when Adam sinned (Genesis 3:15), thousands of years before Jesus was even born. "The zeal of the LORD of hosts will perform this," as Isaiah tells us (Isaiah 9:7), and there is nothing in all creation that can prevent the coming of Christ's eternal kingdom.

This is more than a theological concept; it is glorious news that should fill a Christian's heart with rejoicing. Jesus will one day return and establish His eternal kingdom on earth—a kingdom that is characterized by justice and righteousness—and, in the words of Handel's grand chorus, "He shall reign forever and ever." This is a foregone conclusion to world history. God the Father established this plan even before He set about creating the entire universe. Indeed, one could consider the entire history of the universe as being a forerunner to the establishment of Christ's eternal kingdom, and God's sovereign hand has been guiding and directing all events toward that end since the day He created Adam and Eve.

This anticipation can be a source of comfort and strength during times of suffering or hardship, and it can also be a challenge to strive for greater holiness. Jesus will "rule all nations with a rod of iron" (Revelation 12:5), indicating His aversion to all forms of wickedness. Those whom He has redeemed will never face the eternal wrath of God, yet Christians in particular ought to shun anything that God hates. Christ's eternal rule is an absolute guarantee, and it is wise for His redeemed to prepare for that day in advance by purifying our lives from sinful behavior.

The Woman and the Dragon

But the woman was given two wings of a great eagle, that she might fly into the wilderness to her place, where she is nourished for a time and times and half a time, from the presence of the serpent.

—Revelation 12:14

SCRIPTURE: *Matthew 2*

In addition to the signs of the woman and the Child, the vision of Revelation 12 reveals the arch-adversary of God and His people: "And another sign appeared in heaven: behold, a great, fiery red dragon having seven heads and ten horns, and seven diadems on his heads. His tail drew a third of the stars of heaven and threw them to the earth. And the dragon stood before the woman who was ready to give birth, to devour her Child as soon as it was born" (Revelation 12:3–4).

The failure of the dragon's effort is also recorded in Matthew, in the account of the futile attempt of Herod to destroy the infant Christ (Matthew 2). Instead, "her Child was caught up to God and His throne" (Revelation 12:5) after all things were accomplished concerning the days of His flesh and His resurrection, a statement that is reminiscent of His own words, "I also overcame and sat down with My Father on

His throne" (Revelation 3:21), which were actually fulfilled when Christ ascended.

The vision now carries us to the efforts of the Devil against the Jewish people at the end of our present age. The dragon had been unable to prevent the Son of God from utterly defeating him at Calvary, and he is unable to prevent his everlasting destruction. The dragon's final, pre-millennial effort will be against the nation of Israel, through which Christ became the "male Child."

The subject of the woman's flight and of the efforts of the dragon is continued in Revelation 12:13. Verses 7 through 12 indicate the time of these events. Those verses describe Satan—the dragon—being cast out of the heavenly places, where his activities are still partly carried on (Ephesians 6:12). Since his energies will then be confined to the earth, its godless inhabitants will be given over to the last pre-millennial woes, and a great voice in heaven declares that the time of the kingdom of God and the authority of His Christ has come.

↣ DRAGON ↣

The word translated *dragon* denoted a mythical monster and also a large serpent, so called because of its keen power of sight (from a root word meaning "to see"). Twelve times in Revelation it is used of the Devil.

That proclamation is a time-indicator. The flight of the woman is to take place during the Great Tribulation. The godly remnant of Israel living at that time are here represented by the symbol of the woman, and they will be preserved alive through the time of extreme national distress and peril under the dragon's persecution. Then the woman will flee to the wilderness, as previously mentioned in Revelation 12:6. "But the woman was given two wings of a great eagle, that she might fly into the wilderness to her place" (Revelation 12:14). God had borne His people "on eagles' wings" when they fled from Pharaoh into the wilderness of Sinai (Exodus 19:4; Deuteronomy 32:12), and the same metaphor describes His care in preserving them from the final fury of Satan. The eagles' wings suggest swift escape and certain deliverance.

The woman is nourished "for a time and times and half a time," a period identical with the 1,260 days of Revelation 12:6. The Great Tribulation is destined to last for this period (Daniel 7:25; 12:7). The time is the same as the latter part of the seventieth week in Daniel 9, or a period of seven years. The "times" referred to are years, which is clear by comparison with Daniel 4:23.

From the beginning of human history, the Devil has been working ceaselessly to hinder God's plans and to destroy men and women, hating mankind as a whole simply because we are created in the image of God. His hatred and fury must be great indeed toward the advent of Jesus, the Man who is also God, and Revelation 12 shows us how the Devil, "that serpent of old" (v. 9), poured forth his anger in an intense form upon the Jews as the time of Christ's birth drew close. The Devil's hatred is not restricted to the Jews alone, of course, and there can be times in the life of any Christian when the constant attacks of the evil one tempt us to become discouraged and overwhelmed. At such times, it is important for a believer to keep in mind the bigger picture of God's sovereign control.

Satan thought that he could thwart God's eternal plan of sending His Son into the world as the Messiah, and in Matthew 2 we see him using all his wiles and wickedness in that attempt. He moved Herod to use the wise men in locating where Jesus was born so that he might murder Him—yet God foiled the Devil's plan by sending the wise men home by a different direction. Then the Devil urged Herod to commit mass murder, hoping to slaughter God's infant Son in the process, but God's sovereign hand once again prevented Herod's plot. God permitted the evil one to bring grievous suffering upon His people at that time, but His holy purposes were not hindered in any way.

We cannot always understand God's purposes in our lives. The Jews living near Bethlehem suffered horribly under the treacherous hand of Herod, as the man who was supposed to protect and lead them wantonly murdered countless innocent boys aged two and under. But what we must remember is that Satan did not accomplish this heinous crime without God's permission. We cannot fully understand God's purposes in allowing the evil one to do such a thing, but we must understand that God was in control, and He never commits evil. God does permit the Devil to bring suffering into our lives at times, but He is doing so for His own eternal purposes—and those purposes are always for our good and His glory.

The Bride, the Lamb's Wife

Then I, John, saw the holy city, New Jerusalem, coming down out of heaven from God, prepared as a bride adorned for her husband.

—Revelation 21:2

SCRIPTURE: *Revelation 21, 22*

We now turn to consider the last of the women mentioned in Revelation. The vision is one of undimmed glory: no adverse power is present, and there is no dark background of suffering or persecution. Here we are brought to the closing presentation of one of the greatest subjects of Scripture, where Christ is seen with His bride in all her beauty and glory. It is His glory that shines in her. His enemy has been hurled to his doom—the dragon, who had sought to prevent her very existence and to thwart the divine purposes of Him who died to make her His own. His subtlety and fierce antagonism have only served to enhance the glory and increase the blessedness of this union and to show forth the power and grace of God who designed it.

It must have been a great relief to John, after all that he had seen in prophetic vision—of upheaval and disaster, of fearful conflict and divine judgments—now to survey the scene of unclouded glory that he describes in the latter part of Revelation chapter 21 and the beginning of chapter 22. One of the seven angels who had emptied the bowls of divine wrath comes to give a message of joy and cheer to John. It was one of those same angels that had shown him the vision of the other woman, the corruptor of the world (Revelation 17:1–3). Then the invitation was, "Come, I will show you the judgment of the great harlot" (17:1); now it is, "Come, I will show you the bride, the Lamb's wife" (21:9). The first time, the apostle was carried away in the Spirit into a wilderness, an appropriate locality for that vision of evil; now he is carried away to a great and high mountain, suggestive of strength, stability, and permanence.

ꕔ BRIDE ꕔ

The Greek word translated *bride* has come into English as *nymph*, and refers to a bride or young wife. It is probably connected with the Latin word meaning "to veil," since the bride was often adorned with embroidery and jewels, and was led veiled from her home to the bridegroom.

We must mount to lofty heights to see the glory of God. It was when Moses and the elders of Israel had come up to the mountain that they saw the glory of the Lord. The dazzling splendor of Christ's transfiguration was to be seen, not down on the plains of earth but on the mountain's height. John was invited to behold the bride, and the angel showed him "the great city, the holy Jerusalem" (Revelation 21:10). How striking is the parallel to the vision of the evil woman, Babylon!

She, too, was presented as a city, "that great city which reigns over the kings of the earth" (17:18). That was Satan's imitation of the pure and virtuous woman: the bride of the Lamb, the heavenly city.

In our last reflection, we considered the horrific evil wrought upon mankind by the enemy of our souls, "that serpent of old, called the Devil and Satan, who deceives the whole world" (Revelation 12:9). We were reminded that Christians need to keep in mind the "big picture," remembering that God is sovereign over all things, and in this chapter, we are given a glimpse of the end of that big picture, when Satan shall be cast down once and forever, utterly destroyed and removed from any interactions with the people of God. This is part of God's plan, conceived before the foundations of the earth, that the enemy should be given license to tempt mankind for a season, but that season shall one day come to an end, and there is no power on earth or in hell that can prevent it.

This fact is a source of great encouragement for the believer who is facing hardship or trials. God does permit the evil one to bring suffering into our lives, but his power is completely limited by God's sovereign control, and God will one day cast him into the pit forever. Today might bring some element of sorrow or difficulty beyond your control, but bear in mind that the day is coming—and coming soon—when all sorrows shall cease. When God's plan for human history has come to completion, He will seize the Devil and his minions and cast them "into the lake of fire and brimstone where the beast and the false prophet are. And they will be tormented day and night forever and ever" (Revelation 20:10).

Until the day when God's plan for human history is complete, God's people can and should expect persecution and hindrance from the enemy of our souls. And he will be all the more diligent as he sees the day approaching. "Woe to the inhabitants of the earth and the sea!" cried a loud voice in heaven. "For the devil has come down to you, having great wrath, because he knows that he has a short time" (Revelation 12:12). Until that day, God's people are called to "let patience have its perfect work, that you may be perfect and complete, lacking nothing" (James 1:4).

Concerning Christ and the Church

Then I, John, saw the holy city, New Jerusalem, coming down out of heaven from God, prepared as a bride adorned for her husband.

—Revelation 21:2

SCRIPTURE: *Genesis 2*

We have to go back to the beginnings of human history to see the first hint of this combination of symbols, the metaphors of both a city and a bride. Let us see what the Genesis record states about the formation of Eve. In the Hebrew of Genesis 2:22, the word that means "to make" is set aside, and a word meaning "to build" is chosen instead: "Then the rib which the LORD God had taken from man He made [literally, *built*] into a woman, and He brought her to the man" (Genesis 2:22).

John's vision in Revelation 21 shows us the application of the metaphor of building the woman who was created to be a helpmeet for Adam, language that anticipated the words of Christ Himself: "I will build My Church" (Matthew 16:18). The same two figures are employed in Ephesians, the epistle that especially sets forth the union of the church with Christ. Paul uses the metaphor of the city in reference to the church in

Ephesians 2:19, and then depicts it in Ephesians 5 as the bride of Christ, the object of His love. He "gave Himself for her . . . that He might present her to Himself a glorious church, not having spot or wrinkle or any such thing" (Ephesians 5:25, 27). The apostle dwells upon the union of husband and wife to complete his illustration of the union between Christ and the church.

✧ LIGHT ✧

The Greek word translated *light* denotes "a luminary" or "light-giver." It is used figuratively to describe believers as shining in the spiritual darkness of the world. It is also used of Christ as the Light reflected in and shining through the heavenly city.

In Revelation 21, the bride, the Lamb's wife, is also seen as "the great city, the holy Jerusalem, descending out of heaven from God" (v. 10)—an organized community, enjoying fellowship and association under the authority of the Lord. The next words, "Her light was like a most precious stone" (v. 11), have frequently been understood as if they referred directly to the light of the city; that is because the word *phōstēr*, which means "light-giver," has been translated *light*. A better translation would be *luminary* or *light-giver*. Christ Himself is in view. He is described in the statement, "Her light[-giver] was like a most precious stone, like a jasper stone, clear as crystal" (21:11). He is the source of her light, and the city owes all her glory to Him. He is the precious stone. The jasper sets forth the various traits of His character in their perfect combination.

The words "clear as crystal" represent one verb in the original and may be translated more literally *crystallizing*; that is to say, the stone is described not merely as clear as crystal itself; it has a crystallizing power. Christ imparts beauty to His redeemed, He makes His church resplendent with His own glory. In shining out upon creation, she reflects His light, setting forth His character and attributes.

Genesis 1 tells us how God made the heavens and the earth. We are told, for example, that He made the firmament (v. 7), He made the sun and moon (v. 16), and He made man (v. 26). The same Hebrew word is translated *made* in each of these verses, and it is translated *yield* in reference to herbs and fruit trees (v. 11, 12). But when it comes time for God to create Eve, we encounter a new Hebrew word, which literally means "to build" (2:22). Whatever the implications may have been during the week of creation, the word choice suggests that there may have been a difference in the way God created Eve, as opposed to His creation process for all other things. When God created Adam, He took some of the clay He had created on the first day and fashioned it into a man. But He then took a piece of that man—a method of creation that He did not employ for any other creature—and "built" it into a woman.

Eve was created to become the wife of the First Adam, and in similar fashion those who are born again are being built up to become the bride of Christ, the Last Adam (1 Corinthians 15:45). God's work in the week of creation can help us to understand the process He is using in preparing the bride of Christ. He called things into existence simply by the word of His command; He spoke, and things came to be. This same instantaneous transformation occurs when a person is born again: we are immediately and permanently transformed from being "sons of Adam" into our eternal state as "sons of God." However, this miracle of rebirth does not change the fact that we are still sinners; we are transformed into eternal life and sonship, but we are not instantaneously removed from the fallen world in which we live.

This step is what takes time; it is the process of "building" that gradually changes us to be more and more like Jesus Himself. In one sense, this process is a cooperative effort, for we share a part in the building up of holiness in our lives. "As He who called you is holy, you also be holy in all your conduct, because it is written, 'Be holy, for I am holy'" (1 Peter 1:15–16). But ultimately, this work of building us into the bride of Christ is in God's hands, for there is nothing that any human can do to make himself like Christ. This work of perfection is God's alone, even though we bear the responsibility of obedience. For in the words of Vine, "Christ imparts beauty to His redeemed; He makes His church resplendent with His own glory."

The City's Temple

And I heard a loud voice from heaven saying, "Behold, the tabernacle of God is with men, and He will dwell with them, and they shall be His people. God Himself will be with them and be their God."

—Revelation 21:3

SCRIPTURE: *John 2*

The book of Revelation mixes two metaphors together to describe Christ and the church, using both a bride and a city as pictures. The city, often referred to as a woman in biblical traditions, is described as "pure gold, like clear glass" (21:18), while the street of the city is "pure gold, like transparent glass" (21:21). The gold exhibits the glory of divine righteousness. The city and the street are free from defilement, showing forth all the perfections of God's character as exhibited in Christ. There is no temple in the city, "for the Lord God Almighty and the Lamb are its temple" (21:22). There is no need to enter a sanctuary, for in that city, God is publicly seen in Christ. For this reason, no created light is required, as from the sun or moon; the uncreated Light of God illuminates the city—"the Lamb is its light." That is to say, the light that shines does so because of the sacrifice of Calvary. The nations of earth will walk by the light of it, and the kings of the earth will bring their glory into it. They cannot bring their material wealth into it, for it is heavenly, but they will acknowledge its glory, submit to its rule, and pay homage to Him whose city it is.

All who have resurrection bodies will have free entry into the city; that is to say, there will be complete fellowship between those who constitute the city itself and those who have access to it. To use the imperfect illustration of an earthly city, the city has permanent residents, or citizens, and it has visitors, who enjoy association with the citizens themselves. Those who have the right to enter into the heavenly city have their names written in the Lamb's Book of Life (21:27).

꒰ JOHN 2:19 ꒱

Destroy this temple, and in three days I will raise it up: This statement was appropriate to Jesus' reference to "the temple of His body" (v. 21), for such His body was. In it shone the abiding *Shekinah*, the glory of the Lord, "For in Him dwells all the fullness of the Godhead bodily" (Colossians 2:9).

The book of Revelation offers a unique glimpse of God's eternal city. A reader might be intrigued by some of its descriptions and surprised by some of the things that are not present. For example, there is no sea (Revelation 21:1), nor is there any need for the sun to illuminate the earth (v. 23). These things are startling enough in themselves, but there is another missing element of far greater significance: there is no temple in God's eternal city (v. 22). The implications of this are profound, for the temple represented God's presence among His people. It was the place where men and women went to worship, and it was the location of the important sacrifices made for sin. Without the temple, there was no hope of anyone approaching God's presence.

Yet Jesus made it clear that one result of His becoming a man was that the temple itself would be done away with. He told the Jews that "in this place there is One greater than the temple" (Matthew 12:6), and He spoke of His resurrection as the event that would inaugurate His role as the temple's replacement. "'Destroy this temple,'" Jesus said, "'and in three days I will raise it up.' Then the Jews said, 'It has taken forty-six years to build this temple, and will You raise it up in three days?' But He was speaking of the temple of His body. Therefore, when He had risen from the dead, His disciples remembered that He had said this to them; and they believed the Scripture and the word which Jesus had said" (John 2:19–22).

Mankind needed a temple, a place to meet with God and to be reconciled to Him, because of sin, which separated us from His holy presence. Yet even the temple was incomplete, because the fellowship men could have with God was very limited. Only the high priest was permitted into God's presence—and that only on limited occasions—and no human was able to look upon His face. But the sacrifice of Christ changed all that, and one day every person who has been redeemed by His blood will enjoy the face-to-face intimacy that Adam knew briefly in the garden of Eden (Genesis 3).

The River and the Tree

And he showed me a pure river of water of life, clear as crystal, proceeding from the throne of God and of the Lamb.

—Revelation 22:1

SCRIPTURE: *Revelation 22*

We have been shown a vision of the city of God, and next the apostle is shown "a pure river of water of life, clear as crystal," which proceeds from the throne of God and of the Lamb. This is apparently symbolic of all the blessings that come from the Father and the Son by the Holy Spirit. Streams of water flow from God's throne, for He is the source of every blessing (Ezekiel 47:1; Joel 3:18; Zechariah 14:8). "There is a river whose streams shall make glad the city of God, the holy place of the tabernacle of the Most High" (Psalm 46:4). Wherever the sovereignty of God is acknowledged, and wherever God is worshiped, there His worshipers receive blessing.

The river refreshes the city itself. Jesus said, "The water that I shall give him will become in him a fountain of water springing up into everlasting life" (John 4:14). The river also flows on to minister refreshment to others, and so it will be the joy of the church to be the channel of blessing to all the subjects of the kingdom of God.

On both sides of the river is the Tree of Life yielding fruit every month. All spiritual fruit comes from Christ. He is the

Tree of Life. There will be no cherubim to block the way, as was the case in Eden after Adam's sin (Genesis 3:24)—the tree will be of free access to all. The divine restrictions laid down in Eden and the curse pronounced when man fell will be forever removed. The fruit of the tree will impart delight and refreshment to all those who constitute the city and to all who have access to it, for Christ will forever continue to minister of Himself to all His saints in glory.

ᗌ ROMANS 5:12 ᗌ

and death through sin: While the "death" in Romans 5:12 refers primarily to the death of the body (as indicated in verse 14), the term may also imply spiritual and eternal death, for these are the consequences of sin, and the surrounding verses point to death as a penalty of sin. Moreover, the life brought to the believer through Christ is set in contrast to death, and this eternal life is more than simply the antithesis to physical death (vv. 12–21).

The Bible is abundantly clear on the origins of death, stating unequivocally that "through one man [that is, Adam] sin entered the world, and death through sin, and thus death spread to all men, because all sinned" (Romans 5:12). Death was not present in God's creation prior to Adam's sin, for God abhors death.

Indeed, death is utterly contrary to God's very nature, for He is Life and in Him is the source of all life (John 1:4; 14:6). This can be seen in the brief glimpse that we are given in Revelation of God's eternal city. It is interesting, as we have already noted, that the sea, whose salt is so frequently associated with human tears, is not present, yet there is still an abundance of water flowing in God's kingdom—the fresh and pure water in the River of Life. And we find here another interesting echo of Eden, where God had planted the Tree of Life along with the Tree of Knowledge of Good and Evil (Genesis 2:9). Adam was given a free choice between life and death (as death came through the knowledge of evil), but in heaven that deadly tree does not even exist. On the contrary, instead of one tree of life, we find at least three in the eternal city—and each of those three trees of life bears fruit, not once a year, but every month! On a purely mathematical level, life is at least thirty-six times as abundant in the city of the Lamb as it was when God first created the earth.

Yet numbers alone cannot convey the sense of life and abundance found in heaven; the mind of man cannot comprehend the fullness of God's grace and love, He "who is able to do exceedingly abundantly above all that we ask or think" (Ephesians 3:20). God's blessings of life and abundance are also not restricted to His eternal city; they are available to all believers here and now. We may not yet be set free from the curse of sin and death in this world, but we have free access into the presence of God nevertheless, and in Him is the source of all life. Jesus touched on this when He taught the Samaritan woman, "Whoever drinks of this water [in an earthly well] will thirst again, but whoever drinks of the water that I shall give him will never thirst. But the water that I shall give him will become in him a fountain of water springing up into everlasting life" (John 4:13–14).

The Lamb and the Stone

Her [light-giver] was like a most precious stone, like a
jasper stone, clear as crystal. . . . But I saw no temple in it,
for the Lord God Almighty and the Lamb are its temple.

—Revelation 21:11, 22

SCRIPTURE: *John 13*

The association of the Lamb and the stone in reference
to Christ is frequent in Scripture. In His relationship to the
church, He is the stone, its strength and stability as well as its
foundation and ornamental splendor, and this is due to His
sacrifice at Calvary as the Lamb of God. Consider the following Scriptures:

- 1 Samuel 7:9, 12, where Samuel first took a lamb for
  the burnt offering as a preparation for victory over the
  Philistines, and then a stone, to which he gave the name
  Ebenezer, as a celebration of victory accomplished;
- Psalm 118:22–27, where the psalmist sings of the sacrifice
  to be bound to the altar and of the stone which is
  become the head of the corner;
- 1 Peter 1:19 and 2:4–7, where the apostle first speaks of
  the value of the precious blood of Christ as of a Lamb
  without blemish or spot, and then of His preciousness
  as the chief cornerstone;

᠅ Ephesians 2:13, 20, which speaks of the union of believers, both Jew and gentile, brought together by the blood of Christ, and then represents them as being built together upon the same foundation, "Jesus Christ Himself being the chief cornerstone."

In God's eternal city, the servants of the Lamb "shall see His face, and His name shall be on their foreheads" (Revelation 22:4). Their capacity to serve then will depend upon their faithfulness now, and their sphere of service then will be determined by their service rendered now. There will be unbroken communion between Him and them, and they will unfailingly show forth His glory, presenting in perfection all the traits of His character. Those who look upon them will at once recognize Christ in them. Finally, those who constitute the city will reign with Christ forever and ever.

᠅ STONE ᠅

The Greek word translated *stone* is used literally for the stones of the ground, for tombstones, for building stones, for idols, and for the treasures of commercial Babylon. It is also used metaphorically for Christ, believers, and for spiritual edification by scriptural teaching.

This beautiful city, then, with all that is set forth in the symbolism of Revelation 21 and 22, is "the bride, the Lamb's

wife." She is to share His sovereign power. How striking the contrast between this closing prophecy, of her reign with Him forever and ever, and that of the woman in chapter 17, who sought to reign over the kings and the inhabitants of the earth in her self-assumed pride and glory! May the wonders of our imminent glory in union with our blessed Lord and Redeemer stimulate us to look for His appearing, and may we present ourselves for service to Him who loved us and gave Himself for us, that He might hereafter present us to Himself, "not having spot or wrinkle or any such thing" (Ephesians 5:27).

In our previous reflection, we considered the fact that all who are redeemed in Christ will one day have free access into God's holy presence, able to speak to Him face-to-face as Adam once did. This eternal and glorious reconciliation of man with God is due entirely to the work of Jesus, God's holy Son, who gave Himself freely to stand in our place, receiving on Himself the full brunt of God's justice toward sin. In this capacity, He is the Lamb of God, the final sacrifice for sin— indeed, the *only* sacrifice that could fully atone for the sin of mankind. God's entire eternal kingdom shall be built upon and ruled over by Jesus, for He is its cornerstone and the rock of our salvation.

And life in God's eternal city will be nothing like the popular notions of heaven, where people float on clouds playing harps. The picture given in Revelation 21 and 22 indicates a bustling city, where countless people come and go freely and with purpose, a place where there is no night, no death, no weeping—a place where God's redeemed spend eternity in joyful and active service to the Lord. "His servants shall serve Him," we are told, "and they shall reign forever and ever" (Revelation 22:3, 5). This is a picture of activity and purpose, not of idleness or boredom.

And that brings us back, once again, to the time we spend here on earth, for our lives here are preparing us for our eternity in God's service. One facet of God's discipline and training in our lives is to prepare us for the areas of service He intends us to fulfill eternally. God's heavenly servants are completely faithful to His will and commands, and perhaps Jesus had this in mind when He taught His disciples to pray, "Your will be done on earth as it is in heaven" (Matthew 6:10). In other words, we prepare ourselves for our eternal service by learning now how to obey Him completely. Without doubt, He had eternity in mind when He washed the feet of His disciples, saying, "If I then, your Lord and Teacher, have washed your feet, you also ought to wash one another's feet. For I have given you an example, that you should do as I have done to you. Most assuredly, I say to you, a servant is not greater than his master; nor is he who is sent greater than he who sent him" (John 13:14–16).

For Further Study

Jezebel

1 Kings 16–21
2 Kings 9
Revelation 2

Babylon

2 Kings 17; 20; 24; 25
1 Chronicles 9:1
2 Chronicles 32:31; 33:11; 36
Ezra 1:11; 2:1; 4:9; 5—8
Nehemiah 7:6; 13:6
Esther 2:6
Psalm 87:4; 137
Isaiah 13:1, 19; 14:4, 22; 21:9; 39; 43:14; 47:1; 48:14, 20
Jeremiah 20—22; 24:1; 25; 27—29; 32; 34—41; 42:11; 43:3, 10; 44:30; 46:2,
    13, 26; 49—52
Ezekiel 12:13; 17:12, 16, 20; 19:9; 21:19, 21; 24:2; 26:7; 29:18, 19; 30:10, 24, 25;
    32:11
Daniel 1:1; 2—4; 5:7; 7:1
Micah 4:10
Zechariah 2:7; 6:10
Matthew 1:11, 12, 17
Acts 7:43
1 Peter 5:13
Revelation 14:8; 16:19; 17:5; 18:2, 10, 21

Martyr

Matthew 18:16; 26:65
Mark 14:63
Luke 24:48

Acts 1:8, 22; 2:32; 3:15; 5:32; 6:13; 7:58; 10:39, 41; 13:31; 22:15, 20; 26:16
Romans 1:9
2 Corinthians 1:23; 13:1
Philippians 1:8
1 Thessalonians 2:5, 10
1 Timothy 5:19; 6:12
2 Timothy 2:2
Hebrews 10:28; 12:1
1 Peter 5:1
Revelation 1:5; 2:13; 3:14; 11:3; 17:6

The Whole

Gospel

Section Contents

Sin

    The Nature of Sin

    Natural Will

    Independence of God

Repentance

    Another Term

    Repentance as Used of God

Redemption

For Further Study

Sin

And when [the Holy Spirit] has come, He will convict
the world of sin, and of righteousness, and of judgment.

—John 16:8

SCRIPTURE: *Romans 6*

The apostle Paul states that the first foundational truth of the gospel is the fact that "Christ died for our sins" (1 Corinthians 15:3). This at once comprises two of the essentials of gospel testimony: the fact of sin, and the death of Christ in relation to it.

The gospel preacher cannot ignore the nature of sin in the sight of God. He has to present the true character of guilt and its divine retribution if he is to proclaim God's love and redeeming grace in Christ. Divine grace is based upon the fact of divine righteousness. The infinite holiness of God is an essential element in the display of His love. In the gospel, mercy and truth meet together; righteousness and peace kiss each other.

The cross casts its solemn light upon the condition of all men and the danger to which sin exposes them. The death of Christ stands through time and eternity as a witness to the character and consequences of sin. This truth was never more needed than in the present day, when popular notions minimize the character of sin and put confidence in the natural impulses of the human heart.

The Spirit of God is here to "convict the world of sin, and of righteousness, and of judgment" (John 16:8)—sin which

- ✑ found its great expression in the rejection and crucifixion of the Son of God;
- ✑ still finds "the offense of the cross" (Galatians 5:11) in the human heart; and
- ✑ has corrupted man so that "those who are in the flesh cannot please God" (Romans 8:8).

✑ SIN ✑

The Greek word translated *sin* means literally "missing the mark," but this etymological meaning is largely lost sight of in the English translation of the New Testament. It is the most comprehensive term for moral trespass. It is used to denote sin as a principle or source of action, or an inward element producing acts, or a governing principle or power.

Many have attempted to make this truth palatable to the natural man, and in so doing have neutralized its power. The faithful minister of Christ will always be on his guard against this.

When teaching someone about the free gift of salvation through Christ, it is always wise to begin by explaining the origin of sin and death, for no one can begin to understand the grace and love of God without first understanding the sinful and hopeless condition of mankind. It is imperative to understand that God created the entire universe to be perfect, free from sin and death. Adam and Eve were created as immortal beings, made in the image of God, having free access into His presence. Indeed, Genesis seems to indicate that God Himself came to earth and walked in Eden on a regular basis (Genesis 3:8). But Adam chose to disobey God's one commandment—a tiny restriction in a world of freedom—and by so doing he alienated the human race from God's presence.

A person must also understand God's abhorrence of sin, a repugnance toward corruption that prevents any sinner from ever entering His presence. And this fact leads directly to the sinless life of Christ, God Himself demonstrating for mankind that obedience to the Creator is the only correct course—even at the price of submitting to death, which was not His due. "For the wages of sin is death" (Romans 6:23), but Jesus had committed no sin and was therefore not subject to death; His voluntary death paid the price that was owed by the human race, a price that no human can ever pay himself: "For by grace you have been saved through faith, and that not of yourselves; it is the gift of God, not of works, lest anyone should boast" (Ephesians 2:8–9).

Finally, a person must understand that there are only two possible options in eternity—to be forever in the presence of God, restored to the perfection and immortality of God's original creation, or else to be cast out of His presence in judgment, enduring the eternal suffering of condemnation. There are no other options: no in-between state, no "make up your own" eternal scheme—and no chance of ever changing your mind. Our modern culture works constantly to deny these basic facts of eternity, denying that there is any such thing as sin or judgment, or attempting to shift the blame onto God for mankind's bondage to death. But without a correct understanding of sin, we cannot hope to understand God's grace.

Sin

The Nature of Sin

Whoever commits sin also commits lawlessness, and sin is lawlessness.

—1 John 3:4

SCRIPTURE: *1 John 3*

Sin is defined by the apostle John as "lawlessness": "Whoever commits sin," he writes, "also commits lawlessness, and sin is lawlessness" (1 John 3:4). *Lawlessness* is the word used, not merely transgression of a law, nor simply its non-observance; it has a far deeper significance. It denotes the denial or rejection of law or restraint, in the spirit of self-will and resistance to God. This is what characterizes sin.

Sin is ignoring divine demands, no matter how the will of God is made known, whether externally, as in the single commandment in Eden, or inwardly, as written on the heart. This attitude of the human heart toward the will of God finds expression in acts of rebellion. Paul testifies to this process in his account of the course of human sin: "And even as they did not like to retain God in their knowledge, God gave them over to a debased mind, to do those things which are not fitting" (Romans 1:28).

Popular ideas concerning sin view it as a misfortune, the product of circumstances, the effect of heredity or environment, or an inevitable stage in human development from a lower plane to a higher plane. Heredity and environment frequently determine the special forms in which sin manifests itself, but such circumstances do not determine the nature of sin in the sight of God. The attempts of the natural mind to account for the existence of sin are often simply a means of finding an excuse for it. The popular view of sin simply makes a distinction between vice and virtue, viewing that which is degrading and immoral as wrong, and that which is uplifting to be right.

ᕽ 1 JOHN 3:4 ᕽ

sin is lawlessness: Sin and lawlessness are different aspects of the same thing. The Gnostics taught that the attainment of knowledge placed a person above moral law, in which case one was rendered neither better for keeping it nor worse for breaking it. The teaching of this passage therefore strikes a blow against such error. The practice of sin is shown to be entirely incompatible with being a child of God.

The human estimate of sin is formed according to certain standards of morality, and these vary. The divine judgment, however, is based upon the unalterable requirements of God

Himself, requirements that are consistent with His own character.

As we've already seen, the world's view of sin is contrary to God's view. The world teaches us that we should indulge our fleshly desires, because denying the flesh leads to bad consequences, such as low self-esteem and false guilt. On one hand, the world claims that there is no such thing as sin, because there is no such thing as absolute truth, no set of regulations that apply universally to all men; on the other hand, the world simultaneously claims that there *is* universal truth, that the one cardinal rule for all men everywhere is to be tolerant and open-minded towards every form of fleshly indulgence.

But there *is* absolute truth. Indeed, the very claim that there is no such thing as universal truth contradicts itself, for the mere claim "there is no such thing" is, in itself, a claim of absolute truth. The world's lies lead inexorably toward self-contradiction and head-spinning inverted logic, and the motive for such twisted thinking lies in the simple determination to nullify God's divine law. At the foundation of lawlessness lies the very sin committed by Lucifer, as mankind's fallen nature never stops declaring, "I shall be my own god!" And if I am my own god, then I alone can determine the difference between right and wrong—for my own life, at any rate.

The world's method of distinguishing between right and wrong is to create artificial definitions of *vice* and *virtue*. Distinctions that ignore God's code of righteousness are the invention of the Devil, and his goal is the same as it was when he was cast out of heaven: to rebel against God and invert His laws in the vain hope of setting himself above his Creator. When a man commits willful sin, he is merely imitating the Devil and practicing the hellish craft of lawlessness.

Sin

Natural Will

For those who live according to the flesh set their minds on the things of the flesh, but those who live according to the Spirit, the things of the Spirit.

—Romans 8:5

SCRIPTURE: *Romans 8*

In every unregenerate person there lurks a will that utterly refuses to submit itself to its Maker, a heart that is dominated by a determination to obey its own impulse and carry out its own inclinations—even beneath much that is virtuous. The innate principle of sin brings all under the same condemnation, and the divine pronouncement embraces all, that "those who are in the flesh cannot please God" (Romans 8:8). Only "the law of the Spirit of life in Christ Jesus" can make us "free from the law of sin and death" (Romans 8:2).

Paul speaks about this universal condition, speaking of mankind in general as "the sons of disobedience." He says, "Among whom also we all once conducted ourselves in the lusts of our flesh, fulfilling the desires of the flesh and of the mind" (Ephesians 2:3). The word translated *lusts* is the ordinary word for "desires," and the word translated *desires* refers to the inclinations of the will. He is speaking not merely of that which is base in the eyes of society but of the inclinations of the natural mind. Paul himself, a person of exemplary morality from his youth with the exception of his persecution of Christians, puts himself in the universal category of "we all."

It is independence of God which constitutes man's nature. For this reason, "the heart is deceitful above all things, and desperately wicked; who can know it?" (Jeremiah 17:9)—"because the carnal mind is enmity against God; for it is not subject to the law of God, nor indeed can be" (Romans 8:7). Unbelief is independence of God, and that is what makes unbelief sin. Unbelief substitutes its own opinions for the Word of God. That is how the apostle describes the sin of Israel: "Seeking to establish their own righteousness, [they] have not submitted to the righteousness of God" (Romans 10:3).

᧱ ROMANS 8:5 ᧱

those who live according to the flesh: That is, those who live in accordance with the dominating principle of the corrupt nature in man.

Faith is the submission of the will of man to the Word of God, the ready acceptance of what God says—called "obedience to the faith" (Romans 1:5; 16:26). In the words of Christ, the great sin of which the world is convicted is that "they do not believe" on Him (John 16:9). If man accepts the word of his fellow man, how much more should he believe the Living God! To prefer one's own thoughts and counsels is the essence of sin—and in this, all men are guilty by nature: "We have turned, every one, to his own way" (Isaiah 53:6).

The essence of sin is a stubborn act of one's will, setting one's own agenda above that of God. Paul speaks of this as "fulfilling the desires of the flesh and of the mind" (Ephesians 2:3), and the word translated *desires* literally means "that which one has determined shall be done." Paul uses the same word in Ephesians 1 when speaking of God's sovereign determinations, His eternal decisions, which He established before the foundation of the earth, "having predestined us to adoption as sons by Jesus Christ to Himself, according to the good pleasure of His *will*. . . . In Him also we have obtained an inheritance, being predestined according to the purpose of Him who works all things according to the counsel of His *will*" (Ephesians 1:5, 11, *italics added*).

When God predestined our adoptions as sons, He made a decree that absolutely would come to pass. When a human being sins, he is in effect attempting to do the same thing, making a sovereign decree that his desires shall come to pass, "come hell or high water." In this, we once again see that sin is the act of setting oneself in the place of God, attempting to set our own will in opposition to God's will. Of course, only God is truly sovereign, and our attempts to usurp His authority will always end in failure. Unfortunately, we can still accomplish much damage to ourselves and others in this process of rebellion.

Sin

Independence of God

*For they being ignorant of God's righteousness, and
seeking to establish their own righteousness, have not
submitted to the righteousness of God.*

—Romans 10:3

SCRIPTURE: *2 Samuel 10*

As we saw in the previous reflection, independence of
God constitutes man's fallen nature. The stubbornness of
the human will constitutes sin and is an affront to the very
sovereignty of God. Hanun, the king of Ammon, mistreated
the messengers sent to him by King David in 2 Samuel 10,
exposing them to shameful indignities. This was more than
an insult to the messengers; it was also an insult to David's
throne. That incident illustrates the true character of sin.
When David himself committed adultery and murder, his
guilt led him to cry out, "Against You, You only, have I sinned,
and done this evil in Your sight" (Psalm 51:4).

God is man's Creator, and as such He has sovereign rights
over His creatures. Yet even so, His every command to men
has man's best interests and welfare at its heart. To refuse His

Word, to reject His counsel, to disobey His dictates, is to insult the throne of God.

✣ ROMANS 8:7 ✣

for it is not subject to the law of God: The tense in this phrase is present continuous, expressing a constant or normal condition. The verb is in the middle voice, signifying the voluntary subjection of oneself to the will of another. The meaning, then, is that the mind of the flesh does not submit itself to the Law of God; it refuses to be controlled by it. What is involved is not mere indifference, but actual hostility.

God made man in His own image, and sin is a dishonor to God, marring that which is the very reflection of His own Being. To disobey His Word is, therefore, to injure oneself. The very words used in Scripture to describe sin help us to understand how wicked sin is in the sight of God. It is falling short of the standard (*hamartia*); overstepping the bounds of God's will (*parabasis*); disobeying His voice (*parakoē*); stumbling instead of uprightness (*paraptōma*); culpable ignorance (*agnoemā*); diminishing what is due (*hēttēma*); transgression of a law (*paranomia*) and the rejection of law (*anomia*); unrighteousness (*adikia*); wandering (*planē*); and so on.

Hanun was a young man who had just become king of Ammon, a neighbor of Israel during David's reign. King David extended a hand of peace and kindness to Hanun, evidently in acknowledgment of some kindness done by Hanun's father. But Hanun's response was one of contempt toward God's people, and he publicly disgraced the messengers whom David had sent, shaving off half their beards and forcing them to walk back to Israel indecently exposed. As we read this account in 2 Samuel, we cannot help wondering what would have prompted Hanun to do such a thing, returning evil for good.

The answer lies in the counsel offered by Hanun's advisers. They were immediately suspicious of David's motives, suspecting that the ambassadors were actually spies. On a human level, this is perhaps understandable, as the king and his advisers were responsible for the safety of their whole nation, and the world of politics is fraught with intrigue and deception. But their great failure came in relying upon their own human wisdom rather than seeking guidance from God, and human wisdom cannot lead a man to righteousness. Quite the contrary, in fact, as demonstrated by these events: human wisdom leads inevitably into sin and foolish choices.

The sin of Hanun was ultimately a sin against God; his insult to the ambassadors was an affront to God's righteousness and sovereignty. Sin, as we have seen, is an act of defiance against God. Our actions might affect other people, but ultimately all sin is directed against God alone. Disobedience to His Word grows out of an attitude that we are independent, that we are not subject to His authority. This pretense of independence forces us to rely instead upon our own wisdom and insights, which is an absolute guarantee of failure. Hanun's response to the ambassadors becomes quite understandable when we recognize that he was simply trying to be independent of God's sovereignty, and his resulting actions give us a clear picture of what we do when we knowingly give in to sin.

Repentance

*If we say that we have no sin, we deceive ourselves, and
the truth is not in us. If we confess our sins, He is faithful
and just to forgive us our sins and to cleanse us from all
unrighteousness. If we say that we have not sinned, we
make Him a liar, and His word is not in us.*

—1 John 1:8–10

SCRIPTURE: *James 2*

Our English word *repentance* has come to signify peni-
tence, remorse, or sorrow for wrongdoing, but the Greek
words translated *repentance* in the New Testament present a
more comprehensive view. In the New Testament, there are
two words translated *repent*: *metanoia* and *metamelomai*. The
two are closely related, but we will deal first with *metanoia*,
and we will deal with *metamelomai* in the next reflection.

Metanoia means "an afterthought," a "change of mind."
The corresponding word used in the Old Testament means
"to grieve over one's action." John the Baptist called the people
to repentance—a change of mind, a confession of sin which
produced a changed attitude toward God. John preached "a
baptism of repentance for the remission of sins" (Mark 1:4),
and that baptism was an evidence of a change of heart toward
God, leading to acceptance of Christ (Acts 19:4).

This change of mind is illustrated in the Lord's words
regarding the people of Tyre and Sidon. Had the works

been done in those cities which were done in Chorazin and Bethsaida, "they would have repented long ago in sackcloth and ashes" (Matthew 11:20–21). The men of Nineveh "turned from their evil way" (Jonah 3:10). That turning to God exactly expresses what repentance is on man's part: changing one's attitude and behavior.

℘ REPENTANCE ℘

In the New Testament, the subject of repentance chiefly has reference to repentance from sin, and this change of mind involves both a turning from sin and a turning to God. The parable of the prodigal son is an outstanding illustration of this. Christ began His ministry with a call to repentance (Matthew 4:17), but the call is addressed to the individual, not to the nation as in the Old Testament. In the gospel of John, repentance is not mentioned, even in connection with John the Baptist's preaching. In John's gospel and first epistle, the effects are stressed in the new birth and in the active turning from sin to God by the exercise of faith.

We have been considering the nature and effects of sin, but we cannot conclude our reflections without also addressing the vital topic of repentance and God's grace. Sin is a lawless condition of willfully setting oneself in opposition to God, attempting to elevate oneself to be equal with God. Repentance, however, is changing one's mind about such matters, coming to recognize that sin is rebellion against God's sovereignty and changing one's attitude to submission to His perfect will.

However, there is another element in repentance besides changing one's mind: changing one's behavior. It is not enough simply to change one's way of thinking; that certainly is the first step, but the second step is equally important. A person's changed attitude must be carried into his behavior; otherwise, that change of attitude is futile. As James warned his readers, "You believe that there is one God. You do well. Even the demons believe—and tremble! But do you want to know, O foolish man, that faith without works is dead?" (James 2:19–20).

This is not to suggest that one's works have anything to do with earning salvation. Paul is abundantly clear on this: "For by grace you have been saved through faith, and that not of yourselves; it is the gift of God, not of works, lest anyone should boast" (Ephesians 2:8–9). Yet, even in this, there is an element of behavior involved in one's salvation: a person must do more than *hear* the gospel, he must *act* on it by accepting God's free gift. In this sense, James' words still hold true, for demons know all about God's free gift of salvation, yet knowing is not enough. Salvation requires true repentance of sin, which involves both changing one's mind and acting on that change.

How much more, then, does this principle hold true for those who have already been redeemed! God promises to forgive our sins the moment we confess them (1 John 1:9), yet that does not mean that we are free to confess a sin and then keep on sinning. Paul addressed this notion in his epistle to the Christians in Rome: "What shall we say then? Shall we continue in sin that grace may abound? Certainly not! How shall we who died to sin live any longer in it?" (Romans 6:1–2). When the Holy Spirit convicts believers of sin, we are called to fully repent of that behavior, first by changing our mind through confession to God and then by changing our behavior.

Repentance

Another Term

For godly sorrow produces repentance leading to salvation, not to be regretted; but the sorrow of the world produces death.

—2 Corinthians 7:10

SCRIPTURE: *Matthew 27*

The second word in the New Testament translated as *repentance* is *metamelomai*, which literally means "to have an after care." This word is found only five times in the New Testament, and is very similar to the other word for repentance (*metanoia*) in its usage. It is said of the son who first refused to go and work in the vineyard (Matthew 21:29); of the refusal of the Jews to believe John the Baptist (Matthew 21:32); of the remorse of Judas in his change of mind after Christ was condemned (Matthew 27:3); of Paul's regret regarding the church at Corinth (2 Corinthians 7:8); and of God Himself in regard to His oath concerning the Priesthood of Christ (Hebrews 7:21).

This word is very similar to *metanoia* in meaning, but a distinction lies in the fact that *metanoia* more specifically refers to the thoughts of the mind, while *metamelomai* refers to the will. *Metanoia* suggests a change of idea, while *metamelomai* suggests a change of care or purpose. This difference is illustrated in 2 Corinthians 7:10, where the apostle says that "godly sorrow produces repentance leading to salvation, not to be regretted" (*ametamēleton*). The change of mind on the part of the saints at Corinth produced freedom from regret. This word is not used with direct reference to the preaching of the gospel.

✵ HEBREWS 7:21 ✵

they have become priests without an oath: There was no place for an oath in the appointment of the Old Testament priests. The temporary nature of that priesthood made an accompanying oath unsuitable. God's oath ratifies the eternal and inviolable nature of Christ's priesthood. Moreover, the descendants of Aaron were priests by virtue of birth and office, while Christ's priesthood has a greatness and glory that are personal.

Yet faith itself involves this change of mind or will, for there cannot be faith without repentance. Faith does not merely involve a realization of one's sinfulness and a change of mind; it goes farther. Faith is the response of the soul to a word from God; it allows a person to receive Christ and the salvation provided in Him. Paul declared that "God . . . commands all men everywhere to repent" (Acts 17:30); he testified "to Jews, and also to Greeks, repentance toward God and faith toward our Lord Jesus Christ" (Acts 20:21). That is to say, he proclaimed the necessity of a change of mind toward God and of the faith which accepts the Lord Jesus Christ.

We do not receive Christ by faith without the change involved in turning from our downward path. Repentance is both from and toward—turning the sinner *from* sin and *toward* God. Preaching the gospel is not simply an appeal to the intellect; men need to be aroused to a sense of their sinfulness in the sight of God. The soil has to be plowed to be ready for the seed. Such stirring of the soul is not of itself repentance; it leads to repentance, and then faith grasps the salvation. When conscience is not aroused to its condition, the hearer may be left in a self-satisfied state, content with the idea that some mere mental exercise has effected entrance into the kingdom. As the apostles said, "Believe on the Lord Jesus Christ, and you will be saved" (Acts 16:31).

There is also a form of repentance that does not lead to salvation, a sense of guilt and remorse that does not lead a person to change his behavior. We can see this most strikingly illustrated in the tragic life of Judas Iscariot, who betrayed Jesus for the price of thirty pieces of silver: "Then Judas, His betrayer, seeing that He had been condemned, was remorseful and brought back the thirty pieces of silver to the chief priests and elders, saying, 'I have sinned by betraying innocent blood.' And they said, 'What is that to us? You see to it!' Then he threw down the pieces of silver in the temple and departed, and went and hanged himself" (Matthew 27:3–5).

Judas's conscience was smitten with remorse for his wicked betrayal of Christ, and that was a good thing. It was a healthy initial response to his sin, and had he acted on it correctly, he would have been forgiven by God. That is to say, had he confessed his sin to God, God would have been faithful and just to forgive him and to cleanse him from the unrighteousness (1 John 1:9). But notice what Judas did instead: he confessed his sin to the chief priests, the very men who had partaken of his sin with him! The chief priests themselves were unrepentant of their sin, and they effectively mocked him for what they probably perceived as weakness, telling him to look after his own sensitive conscience without involving them. But even if they had said, "We forgive you for taking our money to help us murder Jesus," Judas's confession of sin had been made to men rather than to God. His remorse had not led him to a humble change of behavior, submitting himself to the sovereign authority of God.

The repentance that leads to salvation does begin with a sense of guilt, the remorse of a sinful life as experienced by Judas, but it leads to the next vital step of submitting oneself to Christ as the only source of forgiveness for those sins. Jesus illustrated this principle in Matthew 21, telling a story about a man who sent his two sons to work in the vineyard. The first son refused to obey, committing sin, but then repented of that attitude—and went to the vineyard to work. Suppose

---

that this son had experienced remorse for rejecting his father's command, then gone home and apologized—and then gone fishing. In such a case, he would have been experiencing this second form of repentance, a sort of "semi-repentance," feeling guilty but not carrying that repentance into action. When Christians act this way, we are imitating Judas rather than Jesus.

Repentance

Repentance as Used of God

*God is not a man, that He should lie, nor a son of man,
that He should repent. Has He said, and will He not do?
Or has He spoken, and will He not make it good?*

—Numbers 23:19

SCRIPTURE: *Jonah 3*

The word *repentance* is used in the Old Testament, in the book of Jonah and frequently elsewhere, of God Himself. But it must be borne in mind that, when God is said to repent, it denotes simply a change of attitude on His part consistent with His own character and attributes. With Him "there is no variation or shadow of turning" (James 1:17). His immutability, never changing, is set in contrast with man's fickleness. God's relation to man varies with changes in man's character and conduct. The passage in Scripture which most explicitly sets this forth is as follows:

The instant I speak concerning a nation and concerning a kingdom, to pluck up, to pull down, and to destroy it, if that nation against whom I have spoken turns from its evil, I will relent of the disaster that I thought to bring upon it. And the instant I speak concerning a nation and concerning a kingdom, to build and to plant it, if it does evil in My sight so that it does not obey My voice, then I will relent concerning the good with which I said I would benefit it.

—Jeremiah 18:7–10

When the Ninevites turned from their evil way, "God relented from the disaster that He had said He would bring upon them, and He did not do it" (Jonah 3:10). Their change toward Him resulted in a change on His part toward them, and His alteration was consistent with His moral attributes as Judge. "God is not . . . a son of man, that He should repent" (Numbers 23:19). That is to say, any change that God may adopt is never due to those conditions which produce a change in man. Man's repentance is due to the fact that he has done wrong. Not so with God. He is a law unto Himself, and His way is perfect. Any variation in His dealings is not a case of correction but of a different display of His divine virtues.

Jonah is best remembered for his underwater journey in the belly of a great fish (not a whale), but that episode was not the greatest and most dramatic part of his life's story. Nineveh was the capital city of the Assyrian empire, a nation

---

that was noted for its cruelty. When the Assyrians conquered a city, they would impale the inhabitants along the city's streets and perform unmentionable barbarities to the women and children. In Jonah's day, Nineveh was prosperous and wealthy, a huge city surrounded by immense walls that were wide enough for three chariots to ride abreast along the top. Yet this great and powerful city responded immediately and unanimously to the dire words of an unknown, foreign prophet as he walked through its streets proclaiming God's coming judgment.

✧ GOD'S REPENTANCE ✧

In the Old Testament, repentance often refers to a person's change of mind out of pity for those who have been affected by one's actions. The Old Testament form of repentance is attributed both to God and to humankind (Genesis 6:6; Exodus 32:14). This does not imply anything contrary to God's immutability, but that His mind is changed toward a person who has changed.

This in itself was a dramatic miracle, at least on a par with Jonah's undersea trip. For point of comparison, imagine an unknown man from Israel suddenly appearing on the streets of New York City, walking the sidewalks and declaiming in a loud voice, "Yet forty days, and New York shall be overthrown!" Perhaps this man is made all the more fantastic by his appearance, bedraggled and pale from being tossed overboard during a storm and swallowed by a huge fish—but who would imagine the people of New York taking him seriously? Yet, in Jonah's case, the entire city of Nineveh suddenly repented of their wickedness, from the beggar in the street to the king on his throne. The most powerful nation on earth humbled itself in sackcloth and ashes at the mere word of God's prophet.

And yet, this is still not the most dramatic and important event which Jonah records. The most breathtaking aspect of Jonah's ministry is the fact that "God relented" (Jonah 3:10). God is the holy and just Judge of all the earth, and He has absolute sovereign authority over all events. It was fully within His right and power to send judgment upon the people of Nineveh, for their wickedness had gone up before God (1:2)—literally, their wickedness had ascended into God's face—yet He chose to withhold His hand of judgment and send grace and forgiveness instead. God demonstrates this same "repentance" toward every person who humbles himself and repents of sin, relenting of the eternal judgment that is our just due and pouring out eternal life and righteousness and blessings beyond count. There is no miracle or deed or event in the history of mankind that can compare with the grace of God.

Redemption

For you were bought at a price; therefore glorify God in your body and in your spirit, which are God's.

—1 Corinthians 6:20

SCRIPTURE: *Hebrews 3*

In the New Testament, there are two distinct words translated *redeem*, and our English word represents two different ideas. The first is *agorazō*, which means "to buy," with special reference to the actual price paid. By adding the prefix *ex-*, "out of" (*exagorazō*), the word is used of purchasing a slave with the object of securing his freedom. The second word is *lutroō*, which means "to set free," "to deliver." Corresponding to this are the nouns *lytrōsis*, and its strengthened form *apolytrōsis*, which refer to "freeing" or "deliverance." The distinction is obvious between the two sets of terms with regard to redemption. First, there is the payment of the price, and then the actual liberation. In other words, redemption is first by purchase, and then by liberating power.

The apostle Paul twice reminds the Corinthians that they were bought (*agorazō*) with a price (1 Corinthians 6:20; 7:23). The death of Christ was the price paid that they might belong to God and glorify Him in their body, and that they might become the bondservants of Christ and not the bondservants of men.

The apostle Peter warns his readers against false teachers who would bring in destructive heresies, "even denying the Lord who bought them . . . bring[ing] on themselves swift destruction" (2 Peter 2:1). The difference between this word, *bought* (*agorazō*), and the word *lytroō* is particularly important here. It could not be said that these men were redeemed, for they denied the Lord's rights of purchase. Christ paid the price for them (*agorazō*), but only believers are actually redeemed (*lytroō*).

҉ REDEMPTION ҉

Both words addressed here (*agorazō* and *lytroō*) are translated "to redeem." *Agorazō* does not refer to the actual redemption, however, but the price paid for it, while *lytroō* signifies the actual deliverance, the setting at liberty.

Throughout the reflections in this book, we have examined mankind's sinful, fallen nature and considered the fact that no human has any hope of entering the holy presence of God. Yet we would be remiss if we concluded on that note, for the amazing fact is that mankind *does* have hope. Sin and rebellion and a spirit of lawlessness divide unregenerate man from God for all eternity, and no human can ever cast off the curse of death that was placed upon us as descendants of Adam. So God Himself became a man, taking on the weakness of human flesh while retaining the holiness of His own deity. He lived a sinless life in perfect compliance with the will of the Father, thus becoming the Last Adam, fulfilling the obedience to God's commands, which the First Adam so grievously defied.

Jesus voluntarily subjected Himself to death, paying a debt that He did not owe. By doing so, He redeemed the entire human race—redeemed us in the sense of having paid the price for our sins. No human being, from the First Adam to the last person who will one day be born on earth, bore any part whatsoever in this redemption. The price of salvation was paid entirely and in full by God Himself, and the cost of that redemption was incalculably high. As many have said before, salvation is free, but it was not without cost. It is free to all who receive it, but it was bought at the price of God's only begotten Son.

Yet this gift does require one step on the part of all men: the step of accepting it. A gift that is refused is of no value to the one to whom it is offered; indeed, it is no gift at all if it is rejected. No one can become redeemed in the other sense of the word—set free from the bondage of sin and death—unless he first accepts the offer of salvation through God's Son. Jesus has already paid the redemption price; He has already purchased the gift at great expense. It is truly the most terrible tragedy on the part of anyone who refuses to accept that gift, for the only one who loses by that refusal is the person who remains unredeemed. Imagine a convicted murderer on death row, suddenly finding the doors of his cell thrown open and a writ of pardon held out. "Someone else has offered to die in your place," the felon is told, "and you are free to go." What folly of pride it would be if that murderer obstinately remained in his cell, determined to pay the price of his crimes with his own life. That price has already been paid; the criminal gains nothing by trying to pay it again!

Eternal redemption from sin and death is more than just a change of thinking, a matter of head knowledge and theology. It requires the step of faith, the step of accepting God's offered gift of salvation. We have all been redeemed in the sense of the purchase price being already paid, but only those who accept that gift can be truly redeemed into God's eternal kingdom. If you have not yet accepted salvation through Christ, do not wait another moment. "Today, if you will hear His voice, do not harden your hearts as in the rebellion, in the day of trial in the wilderness, where your fathers tested Me, tried Me, and saw My works forty years . . . but exhort one another daily, while it is called 'Today,' lest any of you be hardened through the deceitfulness of sin" (Hebrews 3:7–9, 13).

For Further Study

Sin (*hamartia*)

Matthew 1:21; 3:6; 9:2, 5, 6; 12:31; 26:28

Mark 1:4, 5; 2:5, 7, 9, 10

Luke 1:77; 3:3; 5:20, 21, 23, 24; 7:47—49; 11:4; 24:47

John 1:29; 8:21, 24, 34, 46; 9:34, 41; 15:22, 24; 16:8, 9, 11; 20:23

Acts 2:38; 3:19; 5:31; 7:60; 10:43; 13:38; 22:16; 26:18

Romans 3:9, 20; 4:7, 8; 5:12, 13, 20, 21; 6–7; 8:2, 3, 10; 11:27; 14:23

1 Corinthians 15:3, 17, 56

2 Corinthians 5:21; 11:7

Galatians 1:4; 2:17; 3:22

Ephesians 2:1

Colossians 1:14; 2:11

1 Thessalonians 2:16

2 Thessalonians 2:3

1 Timothy 5:22, 24

2 Timothy 3:6

Hebrews 1:3; 2:17; 3:13; 4:15; 5:1, 3; 7:27; 8:12; 9:26, 28; 10; 11:25; 12:1, 4; 13:11

James 1:15; 2:9; 4:17; 5:15, 20

1 Peter 2:22, 24; 3:18; 4:1, 8

2 Peter 1:9; 2:14

1 John 1:7–9

1 John 2:2, 12; 3:4, 5, 8, 9; 4:10; 5:16, 17

Revelation 1:5; 18:4, 5

Lawlessness (*anomia*)

Matthew 7:23; 13:41; 23:28; 24:12

Romans 4:7; 6:19

2 Corinthians 6:14

2 Thessalonians 2:7

Titus 2:14

Hebrews 1:9; 8:12; 10:17

1 John 3:4

Repentance (*metanoia*)

Matthew 3:8, 11; 9:13

Mark 1:4; 2:17

Luke 3:3, 8; 5:32; 15:7; 24:47

Acts 5:31; 11:18; 13:24; 19:4; 20:21; 26:20

Romans 2:4

2 Corinthians 7:9, 10

2 Timothy 2:25

Hebrews 6:1, 6; 12:17

2 Peter 3:9

Repentance (*metamelomai*)

Matthew 21:29, 32; 27:3

2 Corinthians 7:8

Hebrews 7:21

Redemption (*agorazō*)

Matthew 13:44, 46; 14:15; 21:12; 25:9, 10; 27:7

Mark 6:36, 37; 11:15; 15:46; 16:1

Luke 9:13; 14:18, 19; 17:28; 19:45; 22:36

John 4:8; 6:5; 13:29

1 Corinthians 6:20; 7:23, 30

2 Peter 2:1

Revelation 3:18; 5:9; 13:17; 14:3, 4; 18:11

Redemption (*lytroō*)

Matthew 20:28

Mark 10:45

Notes

_____

_____

_____

_____

_____

_____

_____

Notes

_____

_____

_____

_____

_____

_____

_____

Notes

Notes

_____

_____

_____

_____

_____

_____

_____

Notes

Notes

_____

_____

_____

_____

_____

_____